CHRISTIAN DOCTRINE IN GLOBAL PERSPECTIVE

Series Editor: David Smith

Consulting Editor: John Stott

TITLES IN THIS SERIES

The New Global Mission, Samuel Escobar

The Human Condition, Joe M Kapolyo

Evangelical Truth, John Stott

CHRISTIAN
DOCTRINE
IN GLOBAL
PERSPECTIVE

The Human Condition

**CHRISTIAN PERSPECTIVES
THROUGH AFRICAN EYES**

Joe M Kapolyo

Series Editor: David Smith
Consulting Editor: John Stott

InterVarsity Press
Downers Grove, Illinois

InterVarsity Press
P.O. Box 1400, Downers Grove, IL 60515-1426
Internet: www.ivpress.com
E-mail: mail@ivpress.com

© *Joe M Kapolyo 2005*

InterVarsity Press® is the book-publishing division of InterVarsity Christian Fellowship/USA®, a student movement active on campus at hundreds of universities, colleges and schools of nursing in the United States of America, and a member movement of the International Fellowship of Evangelical Students. For information about local and regional activities, write Public Relations Dept., InterVarsity Christian Fellowship/USA, 6400 Schroeder Rd., P.O. Box 7895, Madison, WI 53707-7895, or visit the IVCF website at <www.intervarsity.org>.

All Scripture quotations, unless otherwise indicated, are taken from the Holy Bible, New International Version®. NIV®. *Copyright* ©1973, 1978, 1984 by International Bible Society. Used by permission of Hodder and Stoughton Ltd. All rights reserved. "NIV" is a registered trademark of International Bible Society. UK trademark number 1448790. Distributed in North America by permission of Zondervan Publishing House.

Cover design: Cindy Kiple

Cover image: Bonhams, London, UK/Bridgeman Art Library

ISBN 0-8308-3302-1

Printed in the United States of America ∞

Library of Congress Cataloging-in-Publication Data

Kapolyo, Joe M.
  The human condition: Christian perspectives through African
eyes/
  Joe M. Kapolyo.
     p. cm.—(Christian doctrine in global perspective)
  Includes bibliographical references (p.   ) and index.
  ISBN 0-8308-3302-1 (pbk.: alk. paper)
  1. Man (Christian theology) 2. Theology, Doctrinal—Africa,
Sub-Saharan. I. Title II. Series.
  BT701.3.K37 2005
  233'.0967—dc22

                                                            2004025511

P	19	18	17	16	15	14	13	12	11	10	9	8	7	6	5	4	3	2	1
Y	19	18	17	16	15	14	13	12	11	10	09	08	07	06	05					

To Anne, my wife,

for her love and companionship

Contents

Series Preface

THIS BOOK IS ONE OF A SERIES TITLED Christian Doctrine in Global Perspective and is being published by a partnership between Langham Literature (incorporating the Evangelical Literature Trust) and Inter-Varsity Press. Langham Literature is a program of the Langham Partnership International.

The vision for this series has arisen from the knowledge that during the twentieth century a dramatic shift in the Christian center of gravity took place. There are now many more Christians in Africa, Asia and Latin America than there are in Europe and North America. Two major issues have resulted, both of which Christian Doctrine in Global Perspective seeks to address.

First, the basic theological texts available to pastors, students and lay readers in the southern hemisphere have for too long been written by Western authors from a Western perspective. What is needed now is more books by non-Western writers that reflect their own cultures. In consequence, Christian Doctrine in Global Perspective has an international authorship, and we thank God that he has raised up so many gifted writers from the developing world whose resolve is to be both biblically faithful and contextually relevant.

Second, what is needed is that non-Western authors will write not only for non-Western readers but for Western readers as well. Indeed, the adjective *global* is intended to express our desire that biblical understanding will flow freely in all directions. Certainly we in the West need to listen to and learn from our sisters and brothers in other parts of the world. And the decay of many Western churches urgently needs an injection of non-Western Christian vitality. We pray that Christian Doctrine in Global Perspective will open up channels of communication, in fulfillment of the apostle Paul's conviction that it is only *together with all the saints* that we will be able to grasp the dimensions of Christ's love (Eph 3:18).

Never before in the church's long and checkered history has this possibility been so close to realization. We hope and pray that this series may, in God's good providence, play a part in making it a reality in the twenty-first century.

John R. W. Stott
David W. Smith

Preface

THE TASK OF WRITING ABOUT HUMAN BEINGS is near impossible. A writer can authoritatively make only specific and subjective statements limited to his or her experience. Beyond that, one is almost totally reliant on what others have said about human beings. So I am very aware of my personal limitations in this attempt. But in the end, I suppose I am simply exploring a subject that fascinates me. In doing so, I am using my lived experience and my understanding of God's Word to put forward some thoughts about the nature of human beings and their cultural environments.

My interests lie generally in the interface between the Word of God and the world of human experience—in particular, Bemba experience.[1] There was a period of my life when I was submerged in an almost purely Bemba cultural context. The only light in the village came from the sun by day and from various fires dotted around the village at night. The only running water was in the river half a mile a way. Engagement with the world outside was minimal. But that did not last. Christianity and the wider world soon permeated my world, and from the late 1950s until relatively recently I have viewed both of these realities largely through the eyes of a "borrowed" cultural milieu. Although I grew up in Zambia, my initial experiences of both Christianity and the wider world were mediated through personal and corporate Zambian experiences of British colonialism, and its educational and other social legacies enshrined in present Zambian life and its social structures.

In what I go on to write I make the first faltering steps in exploring my own world and use perspectives from that exploration as lenses through which to view both Christianity and the wider world. I believe strongly that this is imperative not just for my own development but, in a small way, for the church as a whole.

Many commentators have recognized that there is a massive demographic and cultural shift in the composition of the Christian church. This is borne out by many statistics. What is happening in places like Soweto, Manila and Rio de Janeiro will determine the character of Christianity in fifty years' time. Making sense of those contexts in the light of the Scriptures will help to clarify and establish the identity of the "next Christendom." Christian students of the Bible and culture from the emerging majority church must give themselves wholly to this task. As Andrew Walls says in his paper "Christian Scholarship in Africa in the Twenty-First Century," given at a missions conference in May 2004:

> Cross-cultural diffusion (which is the life blood of historic Christianity) has to go beyond language, the outer skin of culture, into the process of thinking and choosing and all the networks of relationship that lie beneath language, turning them all towards Christ. . . . This is *deep* translation, the appropriation of the Christian Gospel in terms of that culture, down to the roots of identity.

This process will in the end call for a certain rethinking of theological categories—not a reinvention of historic Christian beliefs but a recasting into more culturally friendly categories. Christianity must make a home in the cultures of the southern hemisphere and thereby lose its foreignness, which is the task of making Christ Lord in these parts. Failure to follow this through will lead to confusion, uncertainty and a lack of theological leadership in the principal theaters of Christianity in the twenty-first century.

In what follows I am aware that I may well be raising more questions than answers or perhaps only indicating the lines along which further explorations must follow. I trust that a growing volume of work from Africa, Asia and South America will affirm the global nature of Christianity while at the same time remaining deeply rooted at the heart of each host culture, to the honor and glory of Christ our Lord.

Joe M Kapolyo
All Nations Christian College
July 2004

Acknowledgments

THE GLOBAL CHRISTIAN LIBRARY IS LARGELY a continuation of John R. W. Stott's efforts in encouraging Christian leadership from the churches of the developing world. I want to express my gratitude to "Uncle John," as he is affectionately called in many parts of Africa.

The day-to-day—or rather, year-to-year—work of encouraging writers to keep at it and of organizing writing workshops has fallen to the series editor, David Smith. Many times I have said to David that as he is better able to express the things I was struggling to say, he really ought to have written the book. But David kept on encouraging me, and I am deeply grateful for his friendship, his ready listening ear and his firmness in dealing with less than helpful text or ideas. David is a true encourager, and without his persistence this book might never have seen the light of day.

Phil Duce and the editorial staff on this project have been excellent and very professional in their work, and I am deeply grateful to them for their friendliness, thoroughness and encouragement.

Anne, my wife, and my two daughters, Patricia and Laura, have had to live with this project for some time now. Their comments and interest in the work have spurred me on. My colleagues on the staff of All Nations Christian College have given me tremendous encouragement to keep at it. I also want to thank the many people who have inspired me through their writings, lectures and conversations. Many of their thoughts are reflected in the text of my work, I hope faithfully and fairly.

Above all I want to thank the Lord, who at the right time brought me into a saving knowledge of Jesus Christ his Son, whom I now serve and have done for the past thirty years in youth work, a couple of pastorates and now in theological/missions training.

In acknowledging my debt of gratitude, I do not thereby transfer any responsibility to others for the inadequacies of this finished product. I bear sole responsibility for the whole work.

Selected Bemba Glossary

WHERE I HAVE NOT LISTED A WORD HERE, I have tried to make its meaning clear in the context where it appears.

akaliwa	is in danger of being eaten or will be eaten
amano	wisdom
ekala	lives with or lives in
Lesa	God
lwalile	ate
masako	feathers
nama	meat or plural of *inama* (animals)
nkoko	chicken, cock or hen
nkwale	spurfowl—red-necked *francolinus*
ubukulu	size, largeness, greatness; used in both physical and moral senses

1

Concepts of Humankind
Old and New

POP MEGASTAR MICHAEL JACKSON epitomizes the confusion that exists about what it means to be human. Jackson is both extremely wealthy and hugely popular—so popular that he is like a god, a global icon idolized by millions. One commentator suggests that Michael Jackson started out as a handsome young African American man but after who knows how many plastic surgery operations and up to perhaps $300,000 later, he ended up looking like a middle-aged white woman.[1]

Jackson is an adult with a vivid interest in the make-believe, evergreen, childish world of Peter Pan. He admits to sharing his bed with children, a matter that has landed him in hot water more than once. For a long time, he wore a breathing mask wherever he went, and his children never appear in public without facial masks.

Is this simply paranoia or a loss of identity? If Michael Jackson were the human paradigm, what kind of beings would we turn out to be? What does it mean to be human?

The technological and biomedical advances since the beginning of the twentieth century have been immense. NASA and other space agencies are able not just to send people to the moon and back but to send unmanned probes to Mars, Jupiter and Saturn. Specialists are constantly

pushing the frontiers of knowledge and coming up with new and fasci-
nating knowledge about the universe we live in.

Space exploration is matched by discoveries of the internal workings
of the human body. In the year 2000, President Bill Clinton announced
the completion of the Human Genome Project, which identified all the
genes and DNA segments that regulate how genes express themselves in
our bodies—as well as when they cross from one generation to another.
The completion of this massive project boosted our confidence in our
ability to use science to determine our fate, without having to look to the
"stars" for answers.[2] Each of us may soon be able to walk around with a
CD containing all the information about our genetic make-up.

Dolly the cloned sheep made history in 1997 when she was born in
Scotland. Since the turn of the twenty-first century, scientists have been
able to clone pre-embryonic stem cells. These techniques and the cells
they produce may become helpful in dealing with seemingly incurable
diseases such as Alzheimer's. The techniques used are now so advanced
that there seems little risk of the body rejecting new organs grown arti-
ficially. In the future it will be possible to grow specialized tissue for dealing with defective parts of the brain, the heart, the kidney, the spinal
cords and a whole host of other body organs.

Today we are closer than ever to the time when a human being might
be cloned. The Discovery Channel announced that South Korean scientists had created cloned human embryos to generate stem cells. These biological organs were heralded as "the miracle material that may one day
reverse diabetes, cancer, Alzheimer's and other disorders." The research
is aimed at disease therapy, not at creating a cloned human baby; there
are many scientific hurdles to overcome before such research can ever be
used for humans.[3]

Stem cells are nascent cells that can be coaxed by chemical signals in
the body into becoming different kinds of tissue. The significance of the
achievement by the scientists at the Woo Suk Hwang of Seoul National
University lies in their ability to beat a decades-old problem: the patient's

immune system invariably rejects transplanted tissue as foreign if that tissue comes from another body. "To get around that problem the search is on for cloned embryonic stem cells—stem cells that have exactly the same DNA as the patient, and thus would be accepted by his or her body as friendly rather than hostile tissue."

Stem cell research for therapeutic goals is being encouraged, but the same research for reproductive purposes is discouraged. The UNESCO General Conference, in article 11 of its 1997 "Universal Declaration on the Human Genome and Human Rights," states that "practices which are contrary to human dignity, such as reproductive cloning of human beings, shall not be permitted." There are, of course, some scientific mavericks such as the Italian scientist Severino Antinori, who in February 2002 claimed to have cloned a human being. But by and large this is the position of most of the scientific community, and all the countries of the world agree with this declaration, which prohibits the realization of an ethically unacceptable scientific possibility.

The British government allows research for therapeutic aims but has made it a criminal offense to provide public or private funds for research aimed at reproducing a human being. Similarly in America, federal funds are available for research for curative but not for reproduction purposes. However, the law is silent on the use of private funds for reproductive purposes.[4]

We have good reason to be cautious in the race to reproduce human beings scientifically. Science itself calls us to be cautious: as yet the effectiveness of the techniques and the possibilities of defects are unknown and may well lead to imponderable consequences. We have many examples of human abuse of scientific breakthroughs. The patenting of discoveries gives a lot of power to patent holders and can lead to exploitation of others by unjust laws. The prospect of designer babies, communities, races and so on would confuse the social order. So far every human being is the product of two parents, and the resulting person is unique in every way. What relationships would clones have with the donors of the original cells? We would have to design whole new social orders. Or perhaps these designer people would lead to horrific genocides in a bid to create the perfect world free of "defective" human beings.

So knowledge and ability, however wonderful and useful, and now mostly available to a large number of people through the Internet, does not mean that we now know everything there is to know about ourselves—let alone determine how we are likely to turn out or behave—or that we now can solve all of our problems. We still need to discover how to understand proteins, DNA and their functions even in the simplest form of life.

Biomedicine has always suffered from its propensity to isolate a person and a disease within a person, and to treat these without due consideration to the social environment. Deductions made on that basis, however accurate scientifically, are only partial in their application. Even when we take life in its simplest form, many of our characteristics are polygenic: they require interaction with many other genes.

This is quite apart from the fact that biology is not the only important factor in the development of any person; social context, language, culture and other interpersonal activities all have significant parts to play in what makes a particular individual, culture or civilization. Modesty demands that all we can claim is that knowledge of our biological make-up presents us with a whole variety of potentialities, but the actual will be determined by many other factors not directly affected or related to genetic issues. The human condition is too complex for a simple, reductionist, biological or psychological approach. This is why we must resist the temptation to explain human nature on the basis either of nature or nurture, spiritual or material, social or individual. Human beings are complex, and that complexity must be fully taken into account.

Many people see themselves or define their nature in terms of their roles in society. I often view with amusement the practice among many Zambian ministers of the gospel to add the appellation *Pastor* to their names. When asked to give their names many would include their title of what they do, such as Pastor Malcolm Bwalya![5] The same is true with parenthood. Marriage in Africa is really no marriage unless there are children. We feel dignified when, upon the birth of our first child, all our relatives and acquaintances cease to address us by the use of our name and instead use the term "father or mother of . . ." In later years, the names of grandchildren add even greater dignity.

The desire to have children is great partly because having many children is valuable. A Bemba proverb, *Ubukulu bwa nkoko: masako* ("the size of a chicken is its feathers"), means the greatness of a person is measured by the number of his or her children. Barrenness is seen as a terrible curse in Africa, and people will do anything to get children—even, unfortunately, engaging in extramarital affairs, consulting diviners, or worse still, breaking up marriages and entering into unions in search of children. There are few childless Christian couples who are able to withstand the pressure brought to bear upon their marriage.

The African response to the Cartesian formula "I think, therefore I am" is "We are, therefore I am." The African indicates the value of the community in defining one's existence, whereas the European values individualism. The Cartesian statement looks inwardly to an activity and affirms existence. There is a fear that I may not exist at all; the only assurance is found in the activity of the brain. On the other hand, the African's sense of being and self-worth lies in the existence of the community. Neither of these defining statements includes God, but the African understanding of self involves recognition of other people.

It is interesting that both the African and European definitions for personal existence are not based on roles one fulfills, but neither are they strictly speaking ontological statements. When roles are stripped away, who (and what kind of human being) is this that is left? Sadly, in some cases, once the roles and acquisitions are stripped away, nothing is left. Perhaps this is partly what Jesus meant when he spoke about gaining the whole world and losing one's soul.[6] People who define themselves in terms of roles face the specter of emptiness when children leave home or die, when they are separated from a spouse due to death or divorce, at the onset of retirement, in the case of loss of earnings, or in the event of anything that takes away the externals that have supported their self-definition.

Vardy suggests helpfully that it is important for all people to have a definition of self that is core to their values and that remains constant throughout the changing seasons of life. Using Maslow's sevenfold analysis of human need (physical needs, need for safety, need for loving and belonging, need for esteem, need for knowledge, aesthetic needs and need for self-actualization), he points out that most people spend their lives seeking to satisfy their physiological needs, to find safety from physical dangers and anxieties, to seek solidarity in a community or in a relationship with one partner, and to find acceptance based on achievement in work or some other activity where they have developed competence. Such people's identities are located in externals; take those away and nothing is left.[7]

The implications of this analysis are vital for the way in which we define relationships. Do these consist in merely external loving behavior? I recall listening to a talk show host reminiscing about the celebrities he had interviewed over the years. One of the hardest interviews he had ever conducted was with a highly accomplished actor with an impressive list of acting achievements. During the interview this actor could hardly string two sentences together sensibly. He appeared completely tongue-tied! He wanted or perhaps needed a script in order to speak to another person.

Relationships need more than just loving behavior. They must emanate from deep within, something constant in oneself that results in a self-giving activity. Parents have a great responsibility to bequeath to their children the value of a self defined apart from externals. The greatest form of bankruptcy must be an empty heart, the existence of a void where a heart should have been.

A CHRISTIAN VISION OF HUMAN BEINGS

The Bible is clear in its answer to the question of what a human being is. Chapter two will deal with that answer in detail, but what follows are the main points.

Human beings are created by God in his image. Human beings are not God: they are his creatures. There is thus a huge difference between people and God. In Psalm 8 the writer is impressed by the greatness of the universe, the handiwork of God. By comparison human beings are puny and insignificant. And yet God is mindful of these tiny creatures he has made. Although seemingly insignificant, their status in the universe is just a little lower than the heavenly beings who surround the heavenly throne. The human being is crowned with glory and honor.

Such glory and honor includes the majestic godlike abilities and capacities that make up what it means to be created in the image of God—especially the ability to act as stewards, or delegated rulers on God's behalf, over all the creation. Human beings have not always been faithful in their relationship with God; indeed the relationship has been damaged terribly by sin, which permeates every aspect of a person's being. As Genesis 6:5 reports, "Every inclination of the thoughts of his heart was only evil all the time." Sin has penetrated every aspect of human beings, so that even the very origins of the thought process are tainted by sin. This is what in Christian theology is called "total depravity."

The matter is reinforced in the New Testament by such sentiments as "All have sinned and fall short of the glory of God" (Rom 3:23). Sin is like a deep chasm, or an insurmountable barrier that renders impossible any likelihood of a healthy relationship between human beings and God. Instead there is the prospect of a fearful and dreadful end as objects of God's wrath and condemnation (Is 59:2; Rom 6:23; Eph 2:3). The power and effects of sin are shown not just in rebellion (behavior contrary to the will of God) but especially in physical death, which is an analogy of the spiritual death that is the final destiny of human beings in this state of sinful existence outside the will of God.

The Christian's (or rather, God's) solution to this dilemma is the incarnation, which is the coming into the world of Jesus Christ specifically to die, so as to draw the sting of sin, and to rise from the dead, so as to give freedom to all human beings who desire to live in harmony with God in obedience to his will. The provision of God in Christ is available for all human beings through faith; that is, a total belief and dependence on God, trusting that what he has provided is indeed effective. When people put their faith in God's work in Christ, they are said to be born again to a new life with spiritual properties that will continually be evident until, in the eternal presence of God, every vestige of sin will be removed and humans will live together with God in perfect harmony.

Human beings, then, are the pinnacle of God's creative activities. This is a position of responsibility to, rather than anthropocentric indulgent abuse of, the rest of creation. Because of the influence of sin, human beings have fallen to depths of depravity so that, however wonderful our accomplishments, we can never please God. But God has made provision through Christ for all to rise again to newness of life, leading to eternity. This message is for all people, even those who do not belong culturally to the so-called Christian countries.

In order to ensure that this message is heard throughout the world, God called Abraham and, subsequent to and through him, the nation of Israel. Their work was continued and fulfilled by Jesus Christ, who passed on the baton to a small band of twelve disciples through whose efforts the church now exists. Every true member of the church, everyone who has received new life in Christ, is not only a beneficiary of Christ's salvation but a messenger of the good news that Jesus saves. This message is for all people who have not heard. Israel of the Old Testament, many contemporary Messianic Jews, and the church exist to tell the whole world that in Jesus Christ God has done a marvelous thing that will restore humans to the position they first occupied in creation. Christianity is unashamedly on a mission, and there are no areas or cultures that lie outside the sphere of its work.

The Judeo-Christian vision of human beings and life, however, competes with other such visions, including a variety of modernist and postmodern Western views of human beings, along with African and Eastern views. I will give a sketch of some of these views in this chapter and then return to the main theme of this book: the Christian view of the human being.

Over the centuries in the West, many have propounded theories of the nature of human beings. The classical Greek philosopher Plato postulated the theory of unchanging universal Forms and a dualist (body and soul) human nature. The German psychologist Sigmund Freud, well known for his work in psychoanalysis, argued in a firmly deterministic frame that behind every state of being lies a highly significant event or events: all human choices are controlled by hidden causes. This then gave rise to his work concerning *unconscious* mental states, which cannot become evident except by psychoanalysis. He argued too that much of human motivation is driven by a basic sexual instinct.

The best-known French existentialist philosopher, Jean Paul Sartre, born early in the twentieth century, placed the individual human being, in all his or her uniqueness, at the center of life. For Sartre the significant thing about human beings is that we are free to determine the course of our lives. Human beings do not have a fixed state but are always in a state of becoming, which depends on the choices we make. The only truly authentic life is that which is freely chosen by each person for his or her own purpose. For Sartre no external authorities are given to human beings,[8] which is why his philosophy has no place for God. We were not created, nor did we evolve for any purpose. We merely exist. It is a very lonely kind of existence, but we do have to make something of it. Otherwise, a person may decide to commit suicide. Such an action is all right inasmuch as it is a genuine personal decision. Any human being, according to Sartre, is free to make such a decision.

The other two most influential writers on the nature of human beings are Charles Darwin and Karl Marx, who both lived in the nineteenth century. Darwin was an English naturalist who wrote the famous *Origin of the Species*, whereas Marx was a German philosopher responsible for the development of dialectical materialism, which led to communism, the political theory that dominated the world political landscape for much of the twentieth century.

DARWIN'S VISION OF HUMAN BEINGS

Charles Darwin stands as a giant whose shadow directly or indirectly affects all scientific work since the publication in 1859 of his *Origin of the Species*. The bedrock of Darwin's biology is the theory of evolution, the idea that life has developed to its present forms over a very long period of time, stretching back millions of years to a single and simple prototype. Although Darwin is credited with the theory of evolution, others before him had already suggested it, including the geologist Charles Lyell, Darwin's own grandfather Erasmus Darwin, and A. R. Wallace.[9]

Darwin contributed to the theory of evolution by supplying a demonstrable scientific basis for the theory. The evidence he provided was collected from South America, where he acted as a naturalist on an expedition aboard the ship *Beagle*. But perhaps his most telling addition to the theory of evolution was his concept of natural selection, or the survival of the fittest. Plants and animals prey on each other in order to exist. Those quick to adapt to new environments and develop new capacities to adjust to new situations survive better. Although Darwin had set out to study theology and was supported for most of his life by an Anglican financial grant, many people concluded from his work that God was unnecessary in the explanation of the origins of life on earth.

Before Darwin, species were assumed to have a cyclical existence framed by a fixed origin and a final form. The changes that took place did so within this well-ordered frame; distance in time and space seemed not to affect the final form of a species.[10] This was the foundation of the scholastic argument for design. Nature, and especially the species, reflects the idea of order, purpose and perfection, behind which lies an ideal working out of its own eventual manifestation. Although Darwin initially cut across these ideas of fixed forms and purpose, his greater familiarity with both animal and plant life strengthened the argument for design. But his ideas of natural selection finally hit this argument on its head. Organic adaptations and the constant vying and preying on each other of animals did not seem to suggest an intelligent higher being ordering the species.

Contemporary readers will be more familiar with *neo-Darwinist* thought, which extends the arguments to the subject of genetics. Living organisms possess genes that are passed on from one generation to the next. Sometimes characteristics of genes lie dormant for one or more generations, only to reappear later. The sum total of genes in any population of a species is called the gene pool, and evolution is said to have taken place when there is a change in the gene pool. This change can be brought about by a number of factors or mechanisms, including variation and natural selection. By "natural selection" biologists mean that a species or population within a species that has an adaptive advantage, which it is able to pass on to its next generation, will inevitably lead to evolution, a change in the gene pool. This does not mean that individual organisms change but that one part of the population was favored by its adaptive advantage and therefore survived better.

In the "macroevolutionary" scenario all living creatures came into being via evolution from a simple form of bacteria that existed in the sea. (Biochemical science has yet to explain the origins of such living matter. Some scientists postulate that it came to the earth as a form of a virus from somewhere else!) After many millions of years these bacteria began to use the rays of the sun to make sugar, turning carbon dioxide and water into glucose. This increased the availability of oxygen in the sea and in the atmosphere. The bacteria that adapted to the oxygen survived, while the rest became extinct. Different forms of algae evolved, leading to green plants. Animal life came much later, evolving from primitive to sophisticated forms, including the human being, which is distinguished by many characteristics, including its ability to reproduce in its juvenile state.[11]

Darwin's science was in part governed by or based on the foundations of Isaac Newton's physics. Using a reductionist and deterministic approach, Newton maintained that "behaviour of all systems is determined by a few simple laws governing the behaviour of their smallest components."[12] Change in behavior is affected by external influences or pressure such as gravity or atmospheric changes.

Darwin held that survival of the fittest was a key element in the evolutionary process, but survival of the fittest would seem in principle to rule out altruistic behavior, evident especially in human beings. By helping another, an organism is effectively putting at risk its own chances of survival. This is amply demonstrated by the Bemba proverb *uluse: lwalile nkwale* (mercy or helpfulness or altruistic action ate the spurfowl).

A snake was in danger of being engulfed by a bush fire. He pleaded with a spurfowl (a red-necked bird related to quails and partridges) to carry him out of the fire. The bird thought hard and long about the dangers of trusting the snake, but in the end he was overcome by mercy. The snake wrapped himself around the bird's neck, and the bird flew to safety. The snake, however, realized that although he was now safe from the fire, the fire had killed all his potential food. The only way to survive was to eat the spurfowl! And so the bird paid the ultimate price for his altruism.

If survival of the fittest is the norm, then surely humans would not engage in acts of mercy on behalf of others, for this would endanger their own survival. Biologists who want to base any such ethical activity on natural science would argue, as does Richard Dawkins,[13] that genes determine such behavior; in the end mercy will add to the ultimate survival of the population, even if the individual is sacrificed in the process. Likewise, vices have been explained as survival ploys: adultery, for example, ensures the propagation of many more descendants than would be possible in strict monogamy. Concepts of good and bad, it is argued, have the appearance of objectivity but are in fact simply illusions foisted on us by our genes.

The counterargument says that there is a huge difference between biological and psychological selection. It is wrong to attribute terms like *altruism* to lower forms of life with no moral choice. Besides, the transmission of cultural values does not come through one's genetic make-up but through language, tradition, education and social institutions, including religion.[14] There are other materialistic explanations of human beings, such as Karl Marx's dialectical materialism.

MARXIST VISION OF HUMAN BEINGS

Karl Marx was born in Trier, Germany, in 1818 to a Jewish family. His father abandoned Judaism and instead embraced Lutheranism. The conversion was perhaps forced and a humiliating event; politically, Europe was reeling from the shock waves of the French Revolution, which had challenged and changed the government arrangements of France. The nation moved from being a monarchy to being a democracy. The assumed invincible, even divine, power of the kings and queens had been successfully challenged and found wanting.

France was not the only country to be ruled by kings and queens. In a bid to reassert itself, the status quo turned increasingly to the church and biblical passages that affirm the divine origins of authority. In the words of David Smith, "Religion was used to sanctify the traditional structures of society and to curb demands from the oppressed and disenfranchised masses for social reform."[15]

Socially, churches went hand in glove with the current ruling powers. The price of social acceptance, with its economic implications, included conversion to established, state-sponsored churches. The greed, fear and craving for power of the ruling classes were barely disguised by religious pretensions.

These were the concrete political, social and religious dynamics that form the background to Karl Marx's thought and ideology. They may explain the depth of resentment Marx showed toward organized religion in general and Christianity in particular, but perhaps because of Marx's Judeo-Christian background, Marxism is at the same time both radically different from Christianity and remarkably similar.

As a young man Marx attended Berlin University to study law, but in midcourse became increasingly attracted to philosophy instead. The leading philosophers of the time included Georg W. F. Hegel and Ludwig Feuerbach. Hegel is said to have been the greatest of the nineteenth-century German idealists.[16] He held chairs of philosophy at the universities in both Heidelberg and Berlin but died in a cholera outbreak in 1831. His main contribution to philosophy is the idea of historical development: each nation or culture has a personality of its own; this personality is simply a stage of development in a process from what it has been to what it is going to be. In fact, the whole world has just such a personality, which he called an Absolute Spirit. This is patently not the same as the Christian God; rather it is a pantheistic type of god. History, for Hegel, is the progressive "Self-realization" of the Absolute Spirit in the world— the overcoming of alienation in which the Absolute Spirit is confronted by something other than itself.[17] Already one can see the seeds of a dialectical process, where a thesis leads to an antithesis, which is then resolved in a synthesis.

Feuerbach, a successor of Hegel, effectively turned Hegel's basic idea relating to Absolute Spirit and reality on its head. He held that there is one reality: the material world. All religious ideas are fantasies produced by human beings as expressions of alienation or dissatisfaction in the world. God has no objective existence; human beings must be released from the prison house of religion so that they can fully determine their own destiny in the real world. Feuerbach claimed to have destroyed the illusion of religion and paved the path of clear reason, on the basis of which human beings could release themselves from their childish ideas of metaphysical realities.

These were the ideas that captured the imagination of the young Marx at university, and they formed the basis of his own contribution both to sociology and political theory. God was excluded from the universe, and religion was the "opium of the people." In Feuerbach religion was illusory, but in Marx it is a dangerous illusion that blinds one from reality or—more important—from doing something about a bad reality. But the dangerous illusion would not go away simply by education and more knowledge; as long as social contradictions exist, there will be religion. In order to avoid the circumstances (such as religion) that contribute to alienation, one needs to remove—for Marx, only through social and political revolution—the *social* conditions that create the need for religion.

Human beings are productive. Alienation arises from dissatisfaction within the means of existence and might be characterized by a lack of fulfillment in industrial labor. Human consciousness is formed by society, for humans are intensely social beings. History is dialectical: opposing forces resolve in a synthesis, which in turn sets up one force confronting its opposite, leading to a resolution, and so on. Although there was inevitability about this process, Marx allowed for some form of free will, especially in terms of intervention through revolution. Feudalism gave way to capitalism, and capitalism was supposed to give way to communism, which in turn was meant to lead to utopia. But history has not quite worked that way.

Marx's materialist theory of history became very influential. In partnership with Friedrich Engels, Marx set the scene for the establishment of the International Communist Movement, as well as fueling the Bolshevik revolution that saw the overturn of the Russian czars in 1917. The influence of Marxism was most strongly felt in the political and economic arenas, for by the 1970s about a third of the world's population lived under some form of communist-directed government. Within the Christian church, Latin American liberation theology drew its method largely from Marxist thought in its fight against capitalistic structural oppression in Latin American societies. Even in countries where capitalism held sway, many trade union leaders were strongly influenced by communist ideas.

History, however, has had the last word on Marxism. In 1989 the Berlin wall, the most visible symbol of the division between capitalist West and communist East, came tumbling down, and with it communism; outward political and economic forces remain only in China, Cuba and North Korea.

Marx's intellectual contribution continues to exercise the minds of political, economic and social science theoreticians. But did Marx get the nature of human beings wrong? One of the basic flaws in his philosophy was the divorce between the physical and the metaphysical. This certainly made it hard for Africans to embrace communism wholeheartedly. Marx's emphasis on production and the importance of removing alienation from the productive processes was essentially good and not opposed to the biblical concepts of creativity and stewardship. This was his only concession to a concept of universal humanity. Marx's greatest contribution to social science theory is his emphasis on social determinism. Although perhaps overstating the case, he pointed to the formative influence of society on individuals. We are all conditioned by our societies, but even where such conditioning is at its most effective there remains a certain sense of individual agency and universal similarities between human beings quite apart from the obvious biological sameness.

At the peak of communism, there was always the anomaly that communist states were not arriving inevitably from the process of history. Revolution instead tended to come via personal intervention through the barrel of a gun. And in any case these revolutions did not take place in the most industrialized countries, where capitalism not only thrived but brought stability and vast improvements to social conditions as well as a general blurring of the class divisions upon which Marx's theory depended.[18] Marxism nevertheless has given us a good analytical tool for examining societies, although many of its political, economic and religious conclusions have been found wanting. Anyone reading Marx's analysis of society, particularly his charge that religion has masked injustices, will find strong echoes in the writings of the prophets of the

Old Testament (see, e.g., Ezek 16:49; Mal 2:7-9).

Knowledge of God must not lead to ideologies protecting the material, social and political interests of a privileged few, but must lead to action—sometimes costly action—on behalf of the underprivileged, sojourners, aliens, orphans and other people on the margins of society (Mal 3:5). The ethical challenge of Marxist analysis of society must not be allowed to be obscured by Marxist materialist atheism. As Africans in nation-states transform themselves from Soviet-style, "one-party" systems and embrace multiparty democracy based on the secular ideology of market forces, we are in danger of throwing out the proverbial baby with the bath water! Let us not forget that greed, exploitation, social and political elitism do not belong to any one social or political system. These evils are human characteristics that have the capacity to flourish under any guise. Even the church is not immune: churches often shore up egotistical financial and political aspirations of leaders.

UBUNTU: AN AFRICAN VISION OF HUMAN NATURE

Ubuntu or *ubuntunse* is a Bantu ontological noun describing what it means to be a member of humankind.[19] Before the advent of white people in black Africa, the term referred only to black people, but retrospectively it now applies to all human beings. In relation to any one person, *ubuntu* indicates the presence in one's life of such human characteristics as kindness, charity and love of one's neighbor (it thus means the essence of being human, humanness).

Ubuntu describes humans as created by God. There is no independent existence without the creative act of God. Just about all African myths of creation clearly indicate the link between humans and God as their creator and provider of what was needed to sustain life. And yet God, although clearly acknowledged as Creator, is nevertheless not the center of creation. Human beings fill that pride of place, and God is imported, as it were, to explain the origins of *abantu* (people). "[African] ontology is basically anthropocentric: God is the explanation of man's origin and sustenance; it is as if God exists for the sake of man."[20] Similarly, the environment (nature) exists for the benefit of humans and their well-being. In fact, the so-called African traditional religions are not religions in the classic European sense of the word but are the description of the religious acts of *abantu*, whose object may or may not be God.

Remarkably, there appears to be almost universal evidence that a rift is understood between God and human beings, which led to the prevalence of death, loss of happiness, peace and immortality.[21] Characteristically, the explanation is given in terms of what people did to annoy God, what caused him to withdraw from human society: they disobeyed his word, some accident occurred, or there was a division between heaven and earth. There is however, a conspicuous lack of a reversal of this tragic separation of God from his creatures. There is no hint of salvation or utopia in some distant future.

> This remains the most serious cul-de-sac in the otherwise rich thought and sensitive and religious feelings of our peoples. It is perhaps here then, that we find the greatest weakness and poverty of our traditional religions compared to world religions like Christianity, Judaism, Islam, Buddhism or Hinduism.[22]

There are three distinct categories in creation apart from God himself: the realm of the spirits, *ubuntunse*, which includes most but not all human beings (to be human one must demonstrate not only physical but especially certain immaterial attributes as well), and the animal world. *Ubuntu* is distinguished from *ifintu* (things—a category that includes the animal creation) by the fact that humanity is the primary focus of God and that humans share in God's divine nature through the gifts of creativity and intelligence. These two qualities are signs of Godlikeness. Humans and animals have common features such as the possession of a body and the requirement to find food, drink and shelter, to seek security and to bring forth young. It is also reckoned that endemic aggression, whether expressed in argumentativeness, physical brutality or chronic self-centeredness, indicates a loss of basic humaneness and a descent into animalistic behavior. One of the worst things or insults said about a person is that he or she is no more than an animal of the forest, lacking even the basic human intelligence required to walk straight.

A human being is bound in a body, has life (breath), is spirit and possesses *ubumi*—strength, vitality or life force. This life force is more than just brute force; it is a sharing in the creative nature of God and therefore has the ability to originate things, to dominate the lower creation and to influence causes—not in the same way that God creates, dominates and influences but in a derivative sense as befits one created by a higher and fuller force.[23] Human beings grow or diminish in their possession of this vital force and therefore become more human through procreation and especially accession, either to chieftainship or any of the special functionaries standing between human life and the world of the spirits. Childlessness is thus a diminution of this vital force and in general a diminution of one's status in society. A childless person will not be given normal respect in society; on his or her death, rituals will be done to prevent that person's spirit from returning to perpetuate childlessness in the society. Men and women are pressured to dissolve childless marriages because they are not adding value to either the couple or the society in which they live. Single young women are also under inordinate pressure to conceive and bear children, even outside marriage.

People aspire to greater and greater heights of *ubuntu* through the life force gained in certain stages of life, such as circumcision, procreation and accession to positions of traditional leadership. There is seemingly a secretion of spiritual powers that raises such leaders higher in the community hierarchy, leading almost invariably to new names along with increased status.

All this is possible because of the tenacious belief that all life comes from God, himself a spirit being. In the basic cosmology, apart from God there are spiritual powers, invisible to humans, that affect our lives. Some people have the ability to tap into the spirit world and to derive power from that realm to affect, for good or ill, what goes on in material life. From this follows the belief that one's life force is most greatly enhanced, and one's status in the community raised above other ordinary people, if one is able to command such powers. Spirit possession is one of the most common ways to attain such powers and knowledge, along with magic and the ability to manipulate spiritual powers. The powers acquired through spirit possession and magic can be used either for benevolent or malevolent ends, affecting individuals within the community and even the community at large. Such power can be used to protect or harm people, cattle, houses and possessions: a rainmaker may bring rain; a diviner may give knowledge regarding an illness or a death; a practitioner of medicine may give charms to woo a loved one or keep a husband from straying into extramarital sexual liaisons. The darker side of these practices are feared and disapproved of, and are generally practiced secretly.[24]

Other *ubuntu* qualities include the possession of a heart, which is the fountain of feelings, intelligence and speech. These qualities set humans apart from the animal creation. They survive death and are carried on in the living dead (see chapter three, below), in what J. S. Mbiti calls "Zamani"—the long past stretching almost into a lost eternity, in which spirits of the dead exist until there is no one left on earth who remembers them.[25] At that time the living dead (or ancestral spirits) cease to exist in any real sense but instead join the vast and more powerful hordes of divinities.

The living dead are disembodied, but they participate in the life of the community in a variety of ways. Sometimes they come back to life in a physical sense in a new child who bears their name, or they are inherited by a relative of the same sex, through whom they continue to exert influence on the family or community. This, incidentally, is why it is paramount that Africans have large families: there will always be a big pool of labor (for obvious economic reasons) as well as a great number of people to keep the memory of (and thus perpetuate eternity for) the living dead.

M. Mnyandu says that "this large family could preserve more effectively the memory and names of the departed ancestors and relatives, since it is believed that with more numbers there is a corresponding increase in the ability and potential for the immortality of the family members."[26]

There are two categories for the living dead: *imipashi* (the good spirits) and *ifiwa* (the evil or bad spirits). The former were well looked after and died a happy death. They use their new spiritual powers to bless those left in the material world. But those spirits of people who left the land of the living with some grievances have scores to settle and return only to inflict harm upon those toward whom they hold a grudge.[27]

What then is authentic humanity? What are its characteristics? Mnyandu suggests that *ubuntu* is not a pure concept in the philosophical sense but is exhibited through the actions of other members of the family and community.[28] Immediately this indicates the Bantu aversion to individualism, which elevates the individual above the rest of the society. There is a paradox here, in that each person—even a child—is clearly recognized as an individual. That is why the giving of names is so important, especially the "name of the belly button" or, as Tempels calls it, the name of the "interior."[29] However, individuals are a part of a community and are most fully *umuntu* within the hierarchy of the community and the commonwealth of the spirits of the dead ancestors. Any work undertaken is a sphere for communal participation, and the benefits are therefore to be shared by all members of the community, not just by those who have played a part in the success of the work.

This communal orientation is seen from the qualities that are regarded as typical to a true *umuntu*: caring, humble, thoughtful, considerate, understanding, wise, godly, generous, hospitable, mature, virtuous and blessed.[30] The overriding quality is *virtue,* the practice of giving of oneself to the promotion of the good of the community.

All these virtues or values (except for "blessed") are oriented toward others. God blesses, spirits bless, and older people too will bless the young, often using the spoken word and sometimes accompanied by the

ritual use of spittle. Being blessed in this sense almost completely corresponds to the biblical concept *šālôm*, used in many psalms and immor-
talized in the famous Beatitudes of Jesus (Mt 5:1-12). As with the biblical
concept, *ubuntu* is essentially something God bequeaths to a person or
people. In order to express such a gift fully, the possessor will need the
training of the community in virtue so that good deeds and the treatment
of other people as *abantu* (humans) will naturally be self-evident.

All the other virtues are expressive of action a person takes in favor of
other people. Selfishness is not a part of being *umuntu*. One must share
what one has with others—especially with the members of one's family,
clan, tribe and friends. This circle of acquaintances and family is at the
same time inclusive and extremely exclusive; people who fall outside
these circles are not entitled to such caring, hospitality and generosity.
This causes problems for the development of true fellowship in churches
made up of people beyond the bounds of any one tribe. It is probably
also true to say that the relative poverty of the church in the many African situations does not correspond necessarily to the lack of material
wealth but to the fact that the church, its members and the activities pro-
moted therein do not fall within the circle of family, clan, tribe and
friends. It is difficult to explain how such a generous and hospitable people can fail to exercise the same qualities in the church.

So, along with virtue, there are two other overriding qualities of
ubuntu: these include on the one hand community and one's complete in-
tegration into it, and on the other hand the *ubumi* (vital force, strength or
energy) and the means by which such vital force is increased to make the
possessor more powerful. *Ubumi* is a basic ingredient in what it means to
be *umuntu*. Indeed, Tempels calls this the "vital force" and regards it as the
"key principle" in what the Bantu mean when they refer to *umuntu*.[31]

THE PRIMACY OF COMMUNITY

It is difficult to overemphasize the primacy of the community over the
individual.

> Ubuntu is not merely *positive human virtues* [caring, peace-loving, peace-making, generosity, etc.] but the very human essence itself, which lures and enables human beings to become Abantu or humanised beings, living in daily self expressive works of love and efforts to create harmonious relationships in the community and the world beyond.[32]

The prominence or primacy of community does not mean that individuality is abhorred or obliterated. Each person is given a name peculiar to that person. Great care is taken to choose the name, either through the dreams of the expectant mother or some other member of the community, or by divination. The name has to be right;[33] it identifies the bearer either with an ancestor or parents' aspirations, or is indeed a description of the present circumstances.

A Burundian man named his son Mbazumutima. The name is a combination of two words; the first, *mbazu*, means "twice," while *mutima* is the word for "heart" (in the biblical sense: will, emotions and intellect). This child was born during a time when a high number of educated people in Burundi were being eliminated in ethnic cleansing. Sending a child to school could easily be a death sentence. This name would always remind the father to think twice before sending his son to school!

But individuals do not live in a vacuum. They are true *abantu* only when they express *ubuntu* in society. The Bemba say, *umuntu ekala na bantu: uwikala ne nama akaliwa* (a person lives with people: he who lives with animals will be eaten). There are two alternatives for living: among people or away from people among the wild animals of the forest. To call a person *umuntu* is immediately to associate that person with *abantu*, the plural of *umuntu*, in community. Only among other people will a person find security and completeness.

The Scriptures also recognize the importance of community. God says of Adam, the lone human creature, "It is not good for the man to be alone. I will make a helper suitable for him" (Gen 2:18). It is unfortunate that this verse is almost solely associated with marriage ceremonies; in that context it seems to suggest that a person is fully human only if married, that it is not good for single people to remain single. This is patently not true, for even the Lord Jesus himself remained single throughout his earthly life. The accent in these words falls rather on the inappropriateness of being without community, and second, that males and females are complementary.[34]

David Atkinson takes this statement as expressing a fundamental truth about what it is to be human; that is, we are made for fellowship with other human beings. He further says that "one of the disastrous consequences of the Enlightenment . . . was the concentration on the individual as the centre of rational self-consciousness. The end of that road is the misery of the Me-generation."[35] Cartesian dualism led to the isolation of the individual and the separation of facts from values, mind and body, reason and emotion, subject and object. Consequently, communion between beings, whether horizontally or vertically, has become a casualty. Community is fragmented and fractured so that even when people share the same roof, they have little to do with each other. Neighborhoods are generally a collection of houses inhabited by people who do not know each other and care little for one another. Human beings were made for community; true *ubuntu* is only possible among *abantu*.

The process of incorporation or enculturation into the community is achieved both by the natural parent-child relationship (by which the newborn imbibes the values of the mother) and also by training, either through participation by young people in community activities or in ceremonies of circumcision and puberty (see below) and any other teaching opportunities linked with the major passages through life. The process of humanization itself includes language acquisition. An *umuntu* needs to be capable of personal expression. People who are unable to speak are at a great disadvantage in society, and every effort is made to find other ways of communicating with them, including especially lip reading and rudimentary sign language.

A true *muntu* also needs to acquire *amano*. The word is variously translated as "brains," meaning intelligence, wit, common sense, wisdom and especially the ability to get out of seemingly insurmountable situations. *Amano* is sometimes (though rarely) an innate quality: in general, people acquire *amano* from others. Several proverbs of the Bemba illustrate this: *amano: mambulwa* (ask others when in doubt; it is safer to inquire from others in order to have the wisdom to accomplish a task), *amano: ni mbuto balalobola* (wisdom is like good seed; one seeks for it wherever it may be found), *amano: manika* (wisdom is like a meadow by the river—it spreads on both sides of the river; a matter must be thoroughly explored in all its aspects), *amano: yafuma mwifwasa yaingila mu culu* (wisdom comes out of a small anthill and enters into a massive anthill; even children are sources of wisdom). It is imperative that we seek wisdom from all the sources where it may be found.

However, *amano* must conform to the values of the community. So *amano yabuweka: tayashingauka ikoshi* (wisdom on your own will not go round your neck; on your own you do not have what it takes to go far). Similar to the English proverb "Two heads are better than one," or the biblical saying "A cord of three strands is not quickly broken" (Eccles 4:12) is the Bemba proverb: *uutwala pa nsaka: tonoula* (he who takes [it] to the *nsaka* [an open rest hut without walls, where village discussions are conducted, gathering place for the men] will not destroy; one who takes his problem to others will surely find wisdom to prevent acting in destructive ways). So language acquisition is important at least for the purpose of gaining wisdom, without which it is difficult to live life fully as a human.

Young people are also socialized through initiation ceremonies and puberty rites like circumcision. Girls who are put through initiation ceremonies after the onset of puberty enter the ceremony as young, ignorant and innocent—what Richards calls "a calm but unproductive girlhood"—but emerge as women into a "dangerous but fertile womanhood";[36] they are now deemed to be fully grown and completely socialized into their society. Some fundamental change is deemed to have occurred in their "vital force"; they are prepared for marriage and the rigors that will come both in terms of sexual intercourse and the responsibilities of keeping a home. The ceremony itself is an elaborate affair that can last as long as a month and includes separation and isolation from the community, learning the different types of symbols and a "secret" language of married life, acquisition of acceptable social attitudes to marriage, hard work, societal expectations of submission to a husband, the distribution of food to the family, the relation between brother and sister, and so on.

Nelson Mandela describes his initiation into manhood as taking the "essential step in life." He was now ready to take on the whole world, to "marry, set up home and plough my own field. I could now be admitted to the councils of the community; my words would be taken seriously."[37] During a typical Zulu initiation ceremony the male initiate is stripped naked along with his companions as a symbol of transparency to the community, humility, openness and receptivity to the customs and guidance of the elders so as to be properly clothed, nourished and enlightened into the hidden mysteries of Zulu life.

Ubuntu has been given a public role especially in the Truth and Reconciliation Commission led by Desmond Tutu, which sought not revenge but the truth, in order to forgive and receive forgiveness. Sworn enemies confronted each other and laid their murky pasts to rest. However, black on black violence continues in KwaZulu-Natal, not to mention other areas of Africa such as the Great Lakes area of Burundi/Rwanda. But perhaps this can be explained by the priority of relatives and clansmen and women. Some of the qualities of *ubuntu* are universal, although they may have particular importance in African communities in sub-Saharan Africa.

In this introductory chapter I have given examples of the way some people in Europe and Africa view human beings. There are also other views of human nature from cultures in Asia and the Americas that I have not mentioned. In the rest of this book I will look at the way the Christian Scriptures describe human beings.

2

Biblical Perspectives on the Human Condition

ANY DISCUSSION ON THE NATURE OF HUMANITY must invariably begin with God's design for human beings. A discussion of biblical anthropology involves an understanding of the image of God in humans. This is particularly pertinent because the cultural mandate was given in the context of the creation of human beings in God's image (Gen 1:27-31).[1]

THE HUMAN CONDITION

The Bible is unequivocal in its emphasis that to be a human is to be made in the image of God. Although the textual basis for this doctrine is quite slender (Gen 1:26-31; 5:1-3; 9:6-7), its influence in biblical and Christian thought is considerable and is the basic assumption about God's dealings with human beings.[2] It is argued from the fact of its priority at the head of the biblical canon and its application to Jesus (Col 1:15) that "the concept of humans in the image of God illuminates all biblical texts that portray humanity."[3] "The doctrine of the image of God in man is of the greatest importance in theology, for that image is the expression of that which is most distinctive in man and in his relation to God."[4]

The key biblical passage is undoubtedly Genesis 1:26: "Then God said, 'Let us make man in our image, in our likeness, and let them rule over the fish of the sea and the birds of the air, over the livestock, over all the earth, and over all the creatures that move along the ground.'" It has been said that with this passage the creation story reaches its height, its climax.[5] It is as if the creative activity up to this point has been in preparation for the arrival of the human being on the stage of history. This is not to say that we therefore have the freedom to exploit nature for our own selfish ends. We are part of the community of the created order, and God holds us accountable for good stewardship in this as in so many other areas.

The special nature of what is about to be created is also highlighted by the use of a special form of the verb *create*. Some forms have humans for subjects, but one form in particular has God as "its subject and implicit agent."[6] This form is used at several very significant stages in the creation story: Genesis 1:1, 21, 27; 5:1-2. In Genesis 1:1 the verb describes God bringing into being something out of nothing. Then the verb is used when God brings into existence the first forms of conscious life—the sea creatures and the birds of the air (Gen 1:21). The third and fourth uses of the verb each include a threefold repetition of the verb in describing God's creation of human beings (Gen 1:27; 5:1-2). The emphasis is unmistakable: human beings are special because they bear God's image.

The two material words, *image* (Hebrew *ṣelem*) and *likeness* (Hebrew *dĕmût*), imply a similarity between the Creator God and human beings, the apex of his creation. Although different, the words are interchangeable and when used together simply intensify the similarity. The one or the other does not introduce new elements. Human beings not only bear the image of God; they *are* his image. This is a Hebraism in which a word or concept is repeated without the tedium of using the same word twice. The repetition may be used to emphasize, or it may be simply stylistic. Calvin explains this by saying that the distinction certain commentators seek between the two words is in fact "nonexistent." "First, we know that repetitions were common among the Hebrews, in which they express one thing twice; then in the thing itself there is no ambiguity, simply man is called God's image because he is like God."[7] But what this representation, this image, this likeness to God consists of is not so easily discerned, as is clear from the variety of scholarly opinion.

God created human beings in his own image. Where in human beings do we see that image? What evidence does the Bible give of what constitutes the image of God in us? The Bible does not give us any direct explanation of what the divine image consists of. The difficulty of dealing with this question can be demonstrated by asking a different but somewhat similar question; namely, where in the guitar is the music located? Is it in the strings or the body, in the mind or the fingers of the player? I am unsure that philosophically the two questions I am asking are indeed of the same order. But there is a similarity which might aid our quest for understanding. It is the whole guitar that produces music, not just each or some of its component parts.

Similarly, it is the whole person who reflects the image of God, not just a part or several component parts. One commentator suggests that the image of God lies in "the whole complexity of being human, the diversities and distinctivenesses of what it is to be a human being in this world."[8] This includes the body. Some people in the past have made a distinction between the physical and the immaterial part of human beings and then proceeded to suggest that the body is evil, the locus of sin in the human being, and that spirit and salvation relate only to the mind, soul and spirit. This is a travesty of biblical teaching. Human beings are an integral whole, and the body is very much a part of that. The Old Testament does not divide human beings into three parts (body, soul and spirit) or two parts (soul and body).

This is not to suggest that God has a body like we do. When the Bible speaks of God in human terms it is simply a way of saying God is a person.[9] Who God is may be expressed in a form that likens him to human beings, but that is an inability on our part to explain what it means to be God. Our explanation in no way becomes an essential part of his nature. This is a difficulty inherent in the limitations of what it means to be a creature attempting to describe the Creator. The commandment that prohibits making images of God does so on the basis that God is form-less, and no attempt must be made to create images to capture his form—which does not exist. This is quite apart from the danger of the created image assuming in time the totality of what it is meant to repre-sent—that is, what is perceived to be God.

Discussion on the subject of the image of God has a very long history, going back to the church fathers.[10] Only in the twentieth century was there any appearance of a consensus among Old Testament scholars.[11] Most of the prominent commentators from among the early fathers tended to take a "substantialist" view of the image; that is, in some sense, the image is a part of what it means to be human. We may choose to call this an endowment, a gift, a capacity, a quality and so on. This way of looking at the subject preserves the integrity of the image in spite of the Fall.

There were some variations and innovations to this view, however. Irenaeus, for example, who based his contribution on exegetical work, made the distinction between image and likeness. To the word *image* he assigned the essential nature of humanity that did not suffer any violence at the Fall. But to the word *likeness* he assigned our original blissful rela-tionship to God, which was thoroughly corrupted and destroyed at the entrance of sin into human experience. For Ambrose the image was def-initely the soul, while for Athanasius it was rationality. Augustine located the image in the soul, to which belonged memory, intellect and will. These three capacities (note the trinitarian bias) give human beings the ability to remember, to know and to love God. Hall suggests that for Au-gustine the emphasis falls strongly on the "will—its original freedom, its bondage on account of the Fall, [and] its renewal through grace."[12] In this, perhaps, he anticipated the contributions of the Reformers; or more likely, the Reformers reflected his seminal work.

The Reformers on the whole, unlike the church fathers, tended to break sharply with any theology or concept that located the image in some essential capacity of human beings. To understand Luther's reinterpretation of the concept of image, it is important to grasp what Hall calls Luther's "monumental reconstruction of the primary categories of belief." Luther's approach was not essentially dogmatic but biblical. He perceived the importance of relationships in biblical discourse. So for him

> *grace* was not a substance but a deed, a continuing gift-deed of the living God to living creatures; *faith* was not the assent to objectifiable dogmas, or propositions about God, but assent to God's person and presence, an ongoing response of trust . . . the creature's right response to the gift of grace; sin was not a quantitative thing, measurable in misdeeds and wicked thoughts that could be reckoned up, confessed and balanced off through equally quantifiable acts of penance, but rather the abrogation of relationship, turning away from God; *righteousness* . . . became for him the designation of a new and right relationship with God.[13]

Although Luther never really explicitly defines what he would put in place of the displaced substantialist view, he emphasizes the critical nature of a right relationship between Creator and creature if the image is to be meaningful at all. The inference is that in the Fall the image of God disappeared with the entrance of sin into human experience. Perhaps it is more accurate to say that it is the human ability to image God that disappears.

For John Calvin the image of God lies principally in "the soul." In the soul we find not only rationality or understanding but also free will. He strongly deprecated those who indiscriminately extended the image of God in humans "both to the body and the soul," although he would argue that there was not a part of the human being "which was not adorned with some rays of its [divine image]" glory.[14] Calvin's main contribution lay in his analogy of the mirror. The human being is a mirror of God, but only in the act of mirroring God can it be said that human beings image God. The image of God is seen in the obedient human being, whose heart is turned toward the Lord in faith, love and worship.

However, since humans are unable to obey God on account of the Fall, there is effectively no point in talking about an image of God in humans.

It is of great interest to me that Calvin should undermine his otherwise brilliant argument by the unfortunate choice of the mirror metaphor. For a start, in order to perform the work of "mirroring," a mirror must have certain aspects that give it the ability to reflect. A plant does not have those reflective qualities and therefore cannot mirror anything in the conventional sense, although even a plant can reflect in dynamic terms the love and expertise of the gardener responsible for its existence. At this point Calvin is unintentionally smuggling the substantialist argument in through the back door. And clearly a mirror as an inanimate object cannot adequately convey such a rich concept as the image of God. The Reformers are right to see relationship as a key in the whole debate, and therefore metaphors like mirror are far too limited and unhelpful.

Modern writers have moved away from regarding human beings as compositions of many parts and have instead emphasized their essential unity. For some this has led to describing the image in terms of the physical being, the body—although even when seen in this light, the underlying theological understanding was always clear. The physical uprightness of the human being was indicative of our ability to commune with God or to domesticate or control the other members of the created realm. Gerhard Von Rad, a representative of many modern writers, emphasizes the equality between the "spiritual and the intellectual" on the one hand and the "splendour of his bodily form" on the other.[15] Undoubtedly the body is not an unnecessary appendage to the whole discussion, for no expression of true humanity is possible outside the body. Jesus himself clearly demonstrated this fact through his birth and his rising from the dead. Both were done in the human body, and in eternity the Son of God will always have a human form.[16]

Karl Barth, an influential Swiss theologian in the mid-twentieth century and perhaps the greatest systematic theologian of his time, laid great stress on the relatedness (or, to use his word, *confrontation*) of God and the humans he had created. The key analogy for Barth was the institution of marriage, in which the human ability to love and relate was expressed. In fact the image of God was not so much in the human being but in this ability to reciprocate relations with other humans. For Barth the "Thou" and "I" dialogical relationship was vitally important. Vertically, God relates to or dialogues with human beings, and horizontally human beings relate to fellow humans, especially in marriage.[17]

Without falling into the dichotomous view of humans, there are nevertheless two elements to the image of God in humans: the structural and the functional. These have been variously called broader and narrower, formal and material.[18] The two elements must be held together in tension; the one presupposes the other. The fact that I am able to eat food, for example, presupposes that I have a digestive system that allows me to ingest food, digest it, extract nutrients for various bodily functions and then excrete the rest. Function depends on capacity, and capacity leads to function: the two hold together. As Packer says, "God's image must be thought of not just as something static and given, like a tattoo that stays on me whether or not I like it, but also as a condition which is more or less achieved according to how I use my God-given capacities."[19] The capacities lead to and are fulfilled in the functions. Although not explicitly stated yet, the context of Genesis 1 makes clear what is the scope of the image of God in human beings. The qualities will include those qualities that can be seen to be a reflection of what is set out as in effect the image of God himself. To the broader, formal or structural qualities belong relationality, rationality and creativity (there is undoubtedly an endless list but I choose these more basic ones for comment). To the narrower or material aspects belongs competence to take care lovingly of the earth and the other inhabitants on its surface, moral uprightness (because all that God created was good) and, above all, love.

God created human beings with the ability or capacity to *relate*. These qualities are not simply an arbitrary lifeless list. What we have here is a description of the dynamic living and life-giving God. These virtues or his intrinsic attributes he has bequeathed to the equally (in a derived creaturely sense) dynamic living human being.

Being able to relate, then, is what Karl Barth implies by the "confrontation between man and woman." This explanation is exegetically justifiable. In Genesis 1:27 the words "in his own image" are made interchangeable with "male and female"; love is the most characteristic feature of the relationship between male and female.

> Our human sexuality, our maleness and femaleness, is not just an accidental arrangement of the human species, not just a convenient way to keep the human race going. No, it is at the centre of our true humanity. We exist as male and female in relationship. Our sexualness, our capacity to love and be loved, is intimately related to our creation in the image of God.[20]

It is a sad fact that we do not pay sufficient attention to the quality of our relationships. Women in Zambia often describe marriage as the "grit your teeth, grin and bear it" club! We were made for relationships and to relate in such a way as to somehow reflect the relationships of love, confidence, trust and harmony that exist within the Godhead. The peculiar announcement "Let us make man," a departure from the more normal "Let there be," has caused much debate. Does this majesterial statement indicate a discussion between the three members of the Godhead, Father, Son and Holy Spirit? Should we see in this statement something of the doctrine of the Trinity? This is the position Schaeffer takes.[21]

It is fair to say that the three members of the Godhead are involved in creation. In Genesis 1:1-3, the Father is Creator (v. 1); the Spirit is said to be "hovering over the waters" of the formless and empty creation (v. 2); and the Son, as the Word that "God said" (v. 3; cf. Jn 1:1-3), is the agent of creation. All this makes sense to us, however, only because of everything else we know from our understanding of the New Testament. We are reading back into the text what we understand clearly from somewhere else. But what then could this statement mean within its context in the first chapter of the Bible?

Derek Kidner does not invoke the trinitarian theory but instead regards the *self-communing* simply as a plural form of the first-person pronoun, the so-called royal we.[22] C. F. Keil and Franz Delitzsch say that

> no other explanation is left, therefore, than to regard it as [plural of majesty]—an interpretation which comprehends in its deepest and most intensive form . . . the truth that lies at the foundation of the Trinitarian view; that is, that the potencies that concentrated in the Absolute Divine Being are something more than powers and attributes of God.[23]

These potencies would later appear to be the distinct persons of the Trinity.

Another explanation suggests that those addressed include the heavenly court, that is, all the angels who are present and serve before the throne of God. This is normally discounted because whoever is addressed takes part in the creation. But this is clearly not the case, since the following verse reverts to the singular. God created human beings in *his own* image—the members of the heavenly court are not involved in creation. Human beings are made in God's image, not in the image of God and the angels.

D. J. A. Clines, following Barth, suggests that since whoever is addressed takes part in the creation, this points to the Spirit of God, mentioned already in verse 2.[24] The Spirit is elsewhere said to be an agent of creation (see Job 33:4; Ezek 37 [the valley of dry bones]; and Prov 8 [the personification of Yahweh's wisdom]). The "Let us" is therefore not a pompous but empty reflective appeal to self; it points instead to a reality existing in plural form that is later revealed as the persons of the Trinity.

So the phrase "Let us make man" in Genesis 1:26 points not to the so-called royal we, nor to a heavenly court including angels, but to the plurality of persons within the Godhead. The full doctrine of the Trinity appears in the New Testament, but in passages such as these we have the elements of the doctrine in embryo. The ability to relate and do so in harmony and for the benefit of all concerned is the essence of life within the Godhead. So at the core of the Trinity is this undeniable fact of relationships: harmonious relationships. The Godhead is "essentially relational in its very internal being or structure."[25] The fourth ecumenical Council of Chalcedon in the fifth century A.D. did not clearly define the interrelationships within the Godhead but clearly set out the criteria that "would rule out all the possible false answers."[26] We know what it is not, although we cannot clearly define it (perhaps because to have the ability to define the infinite God clearly would require qualities of infinity, which is difficult, to say the least, for finite created beings).

Relationality—the ability to initiate and sustain meaningful relationships—is the key definition, in as far as our language will allow us, of what it means to live in "Trinity." In fact we experience all life through a network or networks of relationships. What makes this possible is the human capacity to love. This is our paradigm, indeed our experience. We were created with the ability to love. Every human being should work hard at establishing and maintaining good relationships with all people and especially those who are nearest and dearest to us, along with those of the household of faith. Xenophobia, tribalism, sexism, racism and superiority complexes of any kind are inexcusable at all times but especially among Christians, for we have a double incentive to ensure good relationships: we not only bear the image of God in creation (Gen 1:27) but are the beneficiaries of the grace of God in redemption (Gal 3:28), the process by which that original image is being restored and perfected.

This ability to relate presumes society. Human beings are social beings made for society. Relationships exist between people who are real. Love is truly evident only in a society of people. Some of these people may be unloving, unlovely and altogether objectionable, but these are the turbulent waters in which love is tried and tested. Solitary confinement is deemed perhaps the severest form of imprisonment precisely because it is so unnatural. When God said, "It is not good for the man to be alone" (Gen 2:18), he was not deploring singleness but affirming society.

In Genesis 2:19-20 Adam, under God's direction, exercises an aspect of his function of "having dominion" over the created animal world by classifying them: this is the significance of giving names. Name-giving in the ancient world, as it still is in many modern non-Western societies, was an important activity. The person giving names was seen to be exercising authority. In Adam's case this was another aspect of his authority over the created order. Once the naming and classifying over, Adam is left on his own. The text says, "But for Adam no suitable helper was found." So the naming was not just an exercise in taking authority; it was also to show Adam his need for human companionship. Men and women need the companionship of other people. This is necessary too for the fulfilment of the mandate to multiply, fill the earth and have dominion over all the rest of creation (Gen 1:28).

It is necessary to point out, in the year that the Anglican Communion (and the rest of the church worldwide) is in turmoil over the first appointment of a practicing homosexual bishop in the United States, that sexual relationships of an erotic nature belong to heterosexual marriage (Gen 2:20-25). This is in part the explanation why God created a woman for Adam, not a man, when seeking to meet the need for Adam's companionship. Same sex or indeed cross-sex relationships not involving erotic intimacy are important and perfectly all right within the human capacity to love. I will develop these aspects further in dealing with love in various biblical presentations in a later section.

We come next to *rationality*. This gift is foundational; it includes the intellect, powers of reasoning, the ability to receive new data and to integrate them into what has hitherto been known, reflection, planning, and decision making. These activities are all linked in some way to the functioning of the mind, although emotions are very important in the use of the mind. In this sense it may be more helpful to employ the word *heart*, which in the biblical usage includes the intellectual faculties (see for instance Mk 7:21, where evil thoughts—a function of the mind—are attributed to the heart). Without the heart it would be impossible to know God, to love him and to love our neighbor as well, to understand our responsibilities and to whom we are accountable vertically or horizontally.

Rationality must also be distinguished from rationalism, a Western philosophical concept in which the mind or reason is privileged over all else. This means that reality is reduced only to those areas that are verifiable through human reason. In relation to religion, rationalism eliminates all experiences of the divine and supernatural from inquiries in epistemology (the way we know things or acquire knowledge), ontology (the way things are) and cosmology (the origins of the universe).

The human intellect is very important to what it means to be human, and it is thus vital—quite apart from health reasons—that we do not surrender our minds to drugs, alcohol or evil spirits. In surrendering our minds we become most unlike God, in whose image we have been made.[27]

Spirit possession is very common among many African people and leads to detrimental supernatural activities, particularly in witchcraft, which devastate whole communities. When a person is fully possessed, the powers at work within their body are not their own. "During the time of possession, one loses his own being, his senses are gone, he is transformed physically and psychologically and becomes simply a tool of the spirit in him. Without realization he acts and speaks according to its wishes."[28] "During possession the individual loses temporarily the control or exercise of his personality, and depicts or mirrors the influence or semi-personality of the spirit or divinity in him."[29] The Gerasenes demoniac of Mark 5:1-20 is a case of a person who through spirit possession became almost subhuman, perhaps even nonhuman, leading an antisocial life contrary to the image of God in him. We surrender our rationality at our own peril. Jesus and his disciples were quick to drive demons out of human beings (see Mk 1:25-26; 3:15; 6:13; Acts 16:16-18).

Rationality is also the basis of science. In Genesis 1 we see order set out from the chaotic and formless mass over which the Spirit of God is said to be hovering (Gen 1:2). From verse 2 to the end of the chapter the creative mind of God gives order to creation. It is this order and the principle of contingence that make science possible. Human rationality is a mirror of the rationality of the Logos of God. It points to a Mind as the ultimate explanation of what lies behind the universe.[30] T. F. Torrance says, "The emergence of scientific knowledge is not something alien to the creation . . . but is part of its proper development and thus a manifestation of its inherent nature and intelligibility, but it is through man and his handling of number and word that this takes place."[31]

Torrance identifies two forms of rationality: number and word. Mathematical formalization, the number type of rationality, is concerned with the measurements of the universe or creation in its impersonal, finite and existential reality. It deals with what can be seen, the tangible and visible aspects of creation. But if this were the whole story (and some scientists seem to give the impression that this is whole story), we would not really be any the wiser about the totality of reality. A pile of bricks is just a pile of bricks, a brute fact which tells no story. Children may turn it into a playground, damaging bricks in the process. But when reference is made to the builder who left it on the building site, the architect who designed the proposed house, the planners who gave permission, the man who wants to build a house for his family, the total cost of the whole project, the picture suddenly changes and the reality into which the pile of bricks fits is different—fuller and more personal. The whole story can really be explained only by exploring all the networks of relationships that are involved in bringing this one project to its desired end.

The other form of rationality, the word, is the process by which human beings transcend the tangibility or mere visibility of inanimate reality to tell the story that lies behind it. It is this part of rationality that makes the connections not only between human beings and their Creator but between people, and between disciplines such as science and theology.

Rationality is therefore a gift of God by which creation, through human beings (themselves a part of the created order), not only discovers itself or continues to discover itself but articulates such discoveries in the context of the purposes of God, whose mind lies behind such intelligibility. Rationality gives us the ability to turn brute facts into personal, understandable and intelligible realities.

Human beings are endowed with the capacity for *creativity*. Human creativity is a truly wonderful spectacle. There seems to be no limit to how creative humans can be. Buildings range from simple but functional mud huts to very complex modern skyscrapers. Vehicles range from the two-wheel bicycle to a modern spacecraft. Clothes range from the simple overalls of a manual worker to intricately woven garments costing hundreds of dollars. In every field of human endeavor—preparing and writing sermons or books, parenting, homemaking, farming, cuisine, arts, crafts and so on—we see demonstrations of great ingenuity. The human capacity to make things and thereby impart value to them is everywhere to be seen. In this we simply reflect the Creator God, whose image we bear; we were made to be like him in the area of creativity.

Human beings should live in an environment in which they exercise this capacity fully. It is demeaning to humanity to create jobs that involve no creativity on the part of the workers. Work must exercise the creative capacity of humans at every level, and education must encourage these creative urges. Where educators are under pressure to get the maximum number of people through exams, education often becomes no more than an exercise in which the mind is turned into an archaic filing system into which more or less useful information is stored with some possibility of retrieval!

Creativity also means that the majority of the people in the world should be producers as well as consumers. But what is produced should be of value both to producer and to consumer. That value should enrich the whole person and not take away people's lives, as do drug trafficking, illicit beer brewing or the sex trade. A specific application of this principle to the church would be for churches to be run by a body of suitably gifted people exercising their gifts for the common good. The church should not be like a bus or an airplane, where the majority of people have come along simply for the ride. Rather it should be like a beehive, where everyone has a significant role to play.

We move now from what capacities we have to what we do with those capacities, how we function. I propose to deal with just two such attributes, including dominion and love.

The first "functional" attribute is *stewardship*, the God-given mandate to rule and have mastery over the rest of creation. For some theologians this is the sum total of what it means to be in the image of God, to be his representative on earth. D. J. A. Clines says:

> That man is God's image means that he is the visible corporeal representative of the invisible, bodiless God; he is the representative rather than the representation. . . . The image is to be understood not so much ontologically but existentially: it comes to expression not in the nature of man but in his activity and function. This function is to represent God's lordship to the lower orders of creation. . . . The dominion of man over creation can hardly be excluded from the content of the image itself.[32]

Clines argues cogently, on both exegetical evidence from the Old Testament and from external evidence culled from the ancient Near East, that the concept of stewardship, while not the sole element in what it means to be made in the image of God, is yet "immediate and necessary" and therefore constitutive of the essential meaning of the phrase "image of God."[33] While accepting the basic strength in Clines's argument, it must be pointed out that people—or things for that matter—function in any capacity on the basis that they have the capacity to do so. Indeed the ability to so function presupposes rationality by which good or bad decisions can be made in the cause of functioning as a representative. It may well be that people are at their most human when they are faithfully being God's representative on earth. It is not, however, necessary to elevate stewardship over the other qualities as the prince of them all.

In theological discourse it has been more normal to use the word *dominion* where I have used *stewardship* (see, e.g., Clines in the quote above). However, dominion has unfortunate connotations, conjuring up massive imperial ambitions generating wholesale servitude of millions of exploited and dominated people. It also raises the specter of the domination of women by men. I suggest that these attributes have constituted abuses of the ability to rule and do not express the intention of God in Scripture.

To understand stewardship one must start with the premise that human beings are God's representatives on earth. This representation is one of responsibility rather than lordship. God is not only the Creator; he is also the one who sustains his creation. Human beings are given the task of ruling as stewards over what God has created, enhancing the environment in which the earth and everything in it flourishes to the honor and glory of the Creator. Such a position of rule "cannot therefore be a lordly and exploitative domination, but a responsible stewardship, a facilitating servanthood, which recognizes that all things derive their existence from God's hands."[34] This cultural mandate speaks of the responsibility of human beings to develop a culture in which the earth and all humanity will flourish to the glory of God.

Stewardship affects our relationship with nature as well as our relationship with fellow human beings. It seems to me that in regard to nature we are to be good stewards, and in regard to each other we are to love in order to avoid mindless exploitation of others. In both spheres our record is not something we can be proud of.

Growing up and living in various townships and villages in Zambia I have observed many a diligent housewife wake up early in the morning and begin the day by sweeping around the house. Traditionally the implement used is a small bundle of spindly twigs about a metre long (in Bemba *umukusao* or *iceswa*), held in one hand and used to sweep dirt. This implement is perhaps too effective: it sweeps all before it, including the layer of topsoil. Every year tons of good topsoil is swept away by hundreds of thousands of overzealous housewives; other sweepers and the rains come and take it all away, dumping it into the rivers, which take it down to the sea. Inadvertently in the cause of cleanliness we aid soil erosion. As the sweeping normally starts at the point of contact between the house and the surrounding area, in time the foundations of the house get exposed; some of the cracks that appear in many houses in the townships are the result of this form of soil depletion. I have banned the use of this implement in the houses I have occupied, and if I was ever in charge of local government I would fight to make production and use of the *umukusao* illegal!

Another form of natural resource depletion is the traditional Bemba form of agriculture, the so-called *chitemene* system. In the dry season a man will select a piece of virgin land with lots of tall trees and will begin not to clear the land for cultivation but to pollard the branches of the trees. Typically a man will cut down trees in this way over an area about six times the eventual size of the garden. The lopped off branches will then be piled high and when completely dry will be set on fire. The resulting ash will be cultivated with the burned soil underneath to provide sufficient soil nutrients for at least one season of growing millet, the staple diet of the Bemba people.[35] The trees and the land will recover over a period of some thirty years, so in some sense this is a renewable resource, and in time the forest will recover. But in the short term and in times of population explosion the devastation of forests is a cause for grave concern. The problem for the Bemba, however, is that there seems no other suitable way to grow millet! No one has "discovered any better method of producing millet in this particular environment up to the present, or even anything as good."[36]

The Bemba people have a proverb, *umusokolobe utwalisha: eo batema* (it is the very fruitful musokolobe tree that gets cut down). The musokolobe tree is a native, wild tree that bears nourishing and delicious fruit. Normally gatherers pick the fruit from the trees, but when they find a tree with an overabundance of fruit, they simply cut the tree down and strip it so that its fruit can be enjoyed by the community. The proverb reflects this tradition but normally is applied to the death of a wealthy person by foul play, so that his or her wealth may be shared by others!

Cutting down the fruit tree reflects an apparent wastefulness and shortsightedness but also a limited anthropocentric and utilitarian attitude which takes for granted that nature is there for our use—we can do with it what we like, when we like. In general in the Zambian case, of course, it is need (and sometimes a little greed and ignorance) that drives the desire to cut down trees; and the exploitation is not wholesale, as certain elements in nature retain a measure of divinization that act to limit wanton destruction.

The European experience is not too dissimilar from the Zambian one, at least in its early developments, before the onset of the Renaissance. Exploitation of nature was expressed in activities arising out of the need for consumption. But the Renaissance changed all that, for attitudes to nature were now driven by a view of humanity that puts nature at our complete disposal. Nature, as it were, was created to meet the needs of human beings. Nature was there not only for our consumption but to meet all our other desires and needs (destruction of thousands of sea animals in order to feed the demands of fashion in the fur trade, the decimation of herds of rhinos in order to use their horns in medicine that addresses human libidinal urges, etc.).

Certain philosophical and scientific changes in Europe led by the rise of rationalism, including the so-called Cartesian dualism, effectively severed the vertical link between human beings and God. This gave humans a position of privilege and unlimited desire for mastery and control over nature, which was reinforced by the apparent success and therefore pride of place of the human being at the apex of the evolutionary chain. These changes were then hitched to the demands of the industrial revolution and the political and imperialist expansionist agendas of the seventeenth to nineteenth centuries.

The results have in some cases been catastrophic. The African slave trade is a case in point. The demand for sugar and cotton for European consumption led to the wholesale displacement, alienation and often decimation of large populations of Africans, the descendants of whom make up the black populations of Latin America, North America and the Caribbean.

What does the Bible say about stewardship? Richard Bauckham suggests four things.[37] First, human beings have delegated authority in nature (Gen 1:26-28; Ps 8:4-8). They represent God and govern nature on his behalf. But what kind of authority is this?

The Bible gives glimpses of the parameters set by God for human exercise of authority in nature. God's own approach to nature is seen as the paradigm for us. He is seen to care for and love "all he has made" (Ps 145:9). The "wonderful works," a euphemism for creation, show the glorious majesty of God and are worthy of meditation (Ps 145:5). In an unwritten language they declare the glory of God (Ps 19:1-4). The Lord is good, compassionate, faithful and loving; he provides food and satisfies the desires of every living thing and all he has made. The emphasis falls heavily on responsibility, caring for and loving everything God has made. His creation is described as "wonderful works"—a phrase used in redemptive contexts. This is how much God cares for his works.

A simple utilitarian attitude to nature robs us of greater riches to be derived from the enjoyment of nature and the God who made it all. It is in the enjoyment of nature that one might experience what C. S. Lewis referred to as "joy."[38] It is a very poor person indeed (perhaps not in material terms) who has ever stood before the *Musi-o-tunya* (literally "the water that thunders"; the Victoria Falls on the Zambezi River on the southern border between Zambia and Zimbabwe) and walked away unimpressed. Most people are overawed by the sheer magnitude of the Falls and, by comparison, the puniness of a single human being in that natural context. The world is full of such wonderful works: Niagara Falls, World View in Matopos in Zimbabwe, Mount Kilimanjaro, the

Rift Valley and so on. God cares for them all and makes provision for their flourishing. We too are called to emulate God in his attitude toward nature.

God's care for nature is also seen in the way Noah is commanded to conserve animals in danger of extinction from the flood (Gen 8). God himself is said to be the preserver of both "man and beast" (Ps 36:6). In Israel there were even legal provisions to insure that the land did not suffer from overuse (Lev 25:1-7).

Second, a body of evidence in the Scriptures shows that human beings have and therefore should preserve strong horizontal relationships with the rest of creation. We are prone to assume a vertical relationship in which human beings are superior to creation, as if we were not a part of creation. In the creation account (Gen 1:26-28) human beings are created along with all the other animals on the sixth day. There are distinctions between human beings and the rest of creation; these include the authority given to human beings to govern creation on God's behalf. But we are still part of the creation and should not lose sight of the solidarity we share with the animals and the rest of creation.

There are many places where God treats us and animals the same, as in the making of the covenant in Genesis 9:8-17. God commits himself to protect against or avoid particular devastating judgments not just for Noah and his children but for "all living creatures of every kind on the earth" (Gen 9:16). In this brief passage the phrase "all living creatures" appears no fewer than five times. Every time Noah is mentioned the phrase "all living creatures" also appears in parallel. The Bible impresses on its readers that the rest of creation has significance to God—not linked to or conditioned by his relationship with human beings.

Similar sentiments are expressed in Psalm 104:9, and it is from God's care of nature that Jesus draws a powerful analogy about depending on God for provision and living within created limits (Mt 6:25-34). Incidentally, one of the lessons Jesus teaches in this passage is that if we minimize our greed and unlimited desire and consumerism, there will be plenty of resources to go around for all on earth.

Third, the epicenter of creation is God the Creator himself, not human beings. Creation is theocentric, not anthropocentric. The climax of the creation story is not the creation of Adam and Eve, however special that was, but God's rest, his glory and his honor. As the *Westminster Shorter Catechism of Faith* says, "Man's chief end is to glorify God and enjoy him forever." The place of human beings in this earth is to bring praise to God and to honor him in what we say and especially in what we do. Similarly, by just being what it is, the rest of creation will bring honor and glory to God. The best worship service depicted in glory includes human beings along with the rest of creation (Rev 4:6-9). Human energies must always be galvanized to bring honor, glory and praise to God our Creator. We do not worship nature, for it is not divine, nor should we destroy, disfigure or abuse it either; rather we should care for it in such a way as to enable it to enter its full potential.

Fourth, what does the Bible see as the ultimate fate of creation? There is a strong human tendency to discard what is no longer useful. The *chitemene* system of agriculture referred to above is a process of using and discarding plots of land and villages. A garden is useful for at the most two or three growing seasons. People and their villages tend therefore to move on in search of virgin land, and nature is left to repair itself. Unfortunately, similar utilitarian attitudes are evident in marriages, where men and society treat women simply as if they were productive gardens, to be "discarded" when they cease to bear children. Often a man will "discard" his wife after many years of marriage simply because she no longer has the appearance of a younger woman. "Use and discard" is the overriding philosophy derived from a strong sense of anthropocentricity.

In church history there have been times when Platonic thought strongly influenced ideas of salvation. The Gnostic movement, for example, conceived of salvation in terms of the escape of the human spirit, the pure human Logos, from the contaminated material body. This sometimes led to libertinism, the idea that one can do whatever one wants to with the body, for the body will not be involved with salvation. At other times it led to asceticism, the idea of imposing a strict and punishing regime to keep the body in check. Any sense of salvation having any kind of solidarity with the material world was deprecated. Similarly the modern vision of life conceives of human beings having total mastery over nature for our own pleasure and glory. Genetic engineering and "designer babies" could easily enhance this potentially destructive vision of the future.

The biblical vision of the future includes reconciliation between humans and nature. Isaiah 11:4-9 features a vision of the end times when, under the leadership of a "shoot . . . from the stump of Jesse," hitherto ferocious elements of nature that would (under normal circumstances) tear each other apart are seen to coexist happily. We catch a glimpse or an echo of this state of affairs in Mark 1:12; Jesus, the shoot from the stump of Jesse, is among wild animals, and angels join in too. The vision finds its culmination in Revelation 21:10—22:5, where nature (notice the reminiscences of the Garden of Eden), human beings and God are reconciled and will live together eternally.

One more biblical reference is instructive in this regard. When God was giving Moses instructions regarding the establishment of a monarchy in Israel, he made it clear that the king would be a brother among brethren (Deut 17:14-20). The king was in no way to put on "airs" as if he were superior. He certainly was not divine, as most of the kings and emperors of the ancient Near East tended to regard themselves. The horizontal relationship with his people was primary. Similarly human beings must not see their relationship with nature as purely vertical but should regard nature with the respect due to a fellow creature.

I began this section on stewardship with a story on housing in Zambian townships and villages; I will end on a similar note. Until 1994, most housing stock in the country was held by either private employers, local councils or the government. The house one lived in was determined by the place one held on the ladder of seniority. Over a period of one's working life, one regularly changed residences in keeping with promotions. The sad thing was that an awful lot of money was spent on housing repairs, because tenants in general did little to add value to the houses they occupied. Lack of ownership may have contributed to the problem, but in general very few people took any pride in the houses they lived in, and unless the owners did everything to maintain the house, it would ultimately fall into disrepair.

It is imperative that we see our role in nature in part as adding value to nature and taking care of it—certainly for our enjoyment but ultimately for the glory of God. It would be intriguing to find out how much this affected the downward spiral in budget deficits all over the developing world.

Before leaving the discussion on stewardship, or rather the abuses of the original command to have dominion, it is imperative that I touch on the domination of women by men. I include this discussion at this point because traditional application of the concept of stewardship as discussed above has been misunderstood and has tended toward the domination and exploitation of nature by humans, mostly men. In human relations, this same tendency of domination has exhibited itself in the near universal domination of women by men along with other forms of inhuman treatment of people, such as exploitation and enslavement.

· The Bemba proverb *abanakashi: mafi ya mpombo* (women are as common as duiker droppings) at its best indicates that there are normally more women in society than men but in general suggests that women do not have much value in society, or rather that their status is inferior to that of men. The proverb is used to calm a young man who seems overanxious to enter into a marriage. In its more sinister meaning it teaches the superiority of men over women, and is used, for instance, by "a disgruntled husband to intimidate his wife or to justify his seeking another wife or an affair because he is displeased with his wife's attitude or performance."[39]

The inferiority of women and their domination by men is confirmed

in various studies conducted by the Women and Law in Southern Africa
Research Trust (WLSA). Unity Dow and Puseletso Kidd, writing from the
context of Botswana, state that the "institution of marriage, as the fundamental social unit, is the pillar of patriarchy. It is the foundation where-
from all forms of male domination over females are born and
reinforced."[40] They cite examples such as marriage negotiations that can
be initiated only by the parents of the suitor. From the onset of marriage
the man's position as "head and guardian" of the family and the subordi-
nate role of the wife are established. Male children are not expected to
do any manual work in the homestead and instead order their sisters
around even when the latter may be in the middle of doing other significant family chores.[41] Women rarely have any rights over property when
issues of inheritance are settled.

Similar examples can be gathered from other African countries. The
older daughter of a university professor was heard to remark that, upon
the birth of her younger brother, he had begun to invest his wealth in
houses and farms. Before his son was born it had not been in his interests
to invest his wealth; he had no one to leave it to. Neither his wife nor his
two daughters had any right to inherit his wealth. Whatever the circumstance, the message is essentially the same: women are not only subor-
dinate to men in society; they are inferior too and as a result suffer all
manner of deprivation, disrespect and sometimes humiliation.

I have often observed, especially in Zambia, that burial arrangements
at funerals will often be made by men with complete disregard for the
women and their views on the matter, even if the burial is that of a husband whose grieving widow is quite capable of making such decisions. It
simply does not occur to the men that the women, especially the widow,
may have useful contributions to make. This domination of women is as
true in the Indian subcontinent, in the Middle East (both Arab and Jewish), and through the West as it is in the Far East. As John Stott says:

> In many cultures women have been habitually despised and demeaned by

men. They have often been treated as mere play things and sex objects, as unpaid cooks, house-keepers and child-minders, and as brainless simpletons incapable of engaging in rational discussion. Their gifts have been unappreciated, their personality smothered, their freedom curtailed, and their service in some areas exploited, in others refused.[42]

But it is not just in contemporary cultures that men show disdain for women. Misogynous statements have come from some unexpected quarters in history. Many of the church fathers had few good things to say about women. Tertullian, who lived from 160 to 220 A.D., is on record as saying that women were the "devil's gateway; the unseeler of that [forbidden] tree; you are the first deserter of the divine law; you are she who persuaded him whom the devil was not valiant enough to attack. You destroyed so easily God's image, man. On account of your desert—that is, death—even the Son of God had to die."[43] Clement of Alexandria called women "a temple built over a sewer"; Jerome asserted that a woman of sound spirituality should be "squalid with dirt" in physical appearance, "almost blind with weeping" in contrition, practicing "continence" in sexual matters, and generally living her life as "a fast."[44]

Unlike these derogatory statements about women and womanhood, the Scriptures unequivocally give men and women dignity and an exalted but equal status. Men and women bear the image of God in equal proportions (Gen 1:26-28). Since the image is described as "male and female" it must mean at least that femininity is represented in God the Creator.[45] The mandate to represent God on earth was given to men and women together, not just men. Genesis 1:28 is very inclusive indeed: God gives both man and woman the same tasks; there is no differentiation based on biological make-up. This is further reinforced when Paul states that as recipients of the salvation Jesus offers, there is neither male nor female (Gal 3:28).

The Bible has a healthy view of women and womanhood. To begin with, God created Eve as the best companion to Adam. Adam and God searched through all the ranks of the created beings to find a suitable companion, but none was found (Gen 2:20). When God did create a companion, it was not another man but Eve, a woman! In his infinite wisdom God determined that the woman was the best companion for the man.

It is common for a boy to be discouraged from being overfriendly with girls. The advice is important to some extent in that many of the chief characteristics that distinguish men and women, in their cultures, are learned when boys and girls develop peer companionship separately and spend lots of time with peers of the same sex. The separation is also supposed to delay the onset of sexual activity between the sexes, although we know that physical separation is not a true barrier to young people if they are determined to engage in sex.

Sexual activity begins early in many societies. The first Anti-AIDS Clubs were set up in Lusaka by Kristina Baker at a secondary school in the early 1980s. It did not take long for Baker, and all the others involved in the fight against AIDS, to realize that Anti-AIDS Clubs needed to be set up in primary schools if they were to have a chance of being successful. By the time boys and girls got to secondary school, most of them (usually fifteen years and older) were already sexually active.

But the separation of the sexes is not only encouraged among the young; it is also encouraged among married people. A clear example of this is seen in the seating arrangements of men and women in many churches, at funerals and even in homes. One side of the church is reserved for men, the other for the women. Same-sex (though not homosexual) companionship is clearly qualitatively more highly valued than marriage companionship. There is no denying that marriage plays an important function, but it is less valued than same-sex peer companionship and even, perhaps especially, biological relationships. "Girls do not enter marriage with any ideal of companionship with their husband. A young couple is not expected to show affection in public and a bridegroom tends to be despised for spending time with his wife. But affection grows over the years in the case of a stable marriage."[46]

The literal meaning of the proverb *Bepa umwanakashi: Umwaume mu-biyo Mukendanankwe* (You may lie to a woman; a man is a friend [companion]—you will walk with him) urges men to tell lies not to fellow men but only to women. The woman (not being a companion) will have no opportunity to verify the facts, whereas a man (being a true companion) will indeed find out the facts. The proverb presupposes that women will not be involved in the world of men—hunting, play and other adventures—but perhaps more significantly, it assumes that the world of women is closed to men and vice versa. All this seems to me to fly in the face of the fact that when God sought to give Adam a "suitable companion" it was a woman he created, not a man. And men and women should not be embarrassed or ashamed or think it strange that they were made male and female. That was the Creator's intention in his infinite wisdom—which is not to deny that there are differences between men and women.

God himself is not ashamed to be described with feminine imagery. We see examples of this throughout the Bible. As has already been discussed, the fact that human beings are made male and female in the image of God means there is something in God's nature that femaleness reflects. To put it bluntly, there are female characteristics in God, as indeed there are in every man. Each of us inherits from our parents sets of characteristics we may suppress, depending on cultural upbringing, but the fact remains that all men bear something of their mother's nature and characteristics. I still recall my maternal grandfather saying about me that I even held the hoe, when tilling the ground, just like my mother had done at my age!

Alongside the Lord's dominant male imagery are a number of female ones.[47] For instance, in the first part of Deuteronomy God is described by Moses using male imagery: "the Rock that fathered you." In typical Hebraic fashion he then repeats the same statement but this time chooses to use female imagery: "the God who gave you birth." Moses knew God in ways most of us can only guess at, yet he was not embarrassed or ashamed and did not consider it heresy to call God the mother of Israel.

Isaiah the prophet also speaks of God as a "woman in childbirth" (Is 42:14), a suckling mother (Is 49:15) and a nursing mother (Is 66:13). David the great king, in describing his sense of security, chooses mother-child imagery: God is the mother and David the child (Ps 131:2; see also Ps 57:1; 61:4). Jesus too likens God to a woman looking for her coins (imagery to show the urgent nature of Jesus' mission and the diligence with which God carries out the task; Lk 15:8-10). We learn from the Gospel writers that when Jesus was approaching Jerusalem for the last time before he was crucified he was filled with compassion for his nation and especially for the city of Jerusalem. He likened himself to a mother hen seeking her brood (Mt 23:37).

Quite apart from female imagery, we must not overlook the significance of the "female narratives," what Richard Bauckham calls "gynocentric" texts, in the Scriptures.[48] Throughout the Scriptures are texts written from the stance of women or the female perspective (though most biblical texts are written from a male perspective). These include Exodus 15:1-21, where the prophetess Miriam, the sister to both Aaron and Moses, leads the women in singing songs of victory. Her prophetic gift is confirmed in Numbers 12 as well as Micah 6:4. The book of Ruth is written from her perspective except for the prologue and the concluding genealogy. Her character as a woman (and a Moabite woman at that) dominates and gives life to the tenor of the narrative. Other such texts include Judges 4—5, the story of Deborah's leadership over Israel, the story and faith of Hannah, which led to the birth and appointment of Samuel, the last judge of Israel and the first prophet of the nation who gave to Israel its first two kings. We also have the Song of Songs as well as the book of Esther, which is set in the Persian imperial city of Susa. In an obviously male-dominated society the voice of this orphan Hebrew girl rings out with courage and diplomacy. Esther's perspective illuminates the narrative, dominating the story in a way that Xerxes', Haman's and Mordecai's perspectives do not.

The New Testament opens with a genealogy peculiar as biblical genealogies go in that it contains names of women. Women were not normally included in genealogies except where they served to distinguish the maternity of two men mentioned in the list.[49] But Matthew includes four Gentile women for no other apparent reason than to show God's favor to these women in drawing them to himself and to the central genealogy of the nation of Israel. Bauckham discusses many other women, including Elizabeth, the mother of John the Baptist, Mary, the mother of Jesus, Anna, the prophetess from the tribe of Asher, Joanna (Lk 8:1-3; Bauckham argues that this Joanna is the same person whom Paul designates an apostle in Rom 16:7), Mary of Clopas, the two Salomes and the witnesses to the resurrection. To these we can add the mother of Mark, whose house became the first building to house the Jerusalem church, Lydia (Acts 16), whose house became the first mission headquarters for Paul's work in Europe, and Priscilla, who with her husband Aquila taught Apollos (Acts 18:26) and through whose hospitality the church in Corinth was born.

The domination of women by men is in part the result of what went wrong in the Fall, when sin affected every relationship. It is also a fact that the predominant influence in Scripture is always male, although God quite clearly breaks through that dominance and allows female voices to ring out, thereby showing his respect for womanhood. Some of the more common arguments used to put down women follow.

First, the idea of *primogeniture*—the belief that since Adam was made first, he is therefore superior to Eve (1 Tim 2:13)—is often cited to support male domination of women. There are two schools of thought in regard to the teaching contained in the latter part 1 Timothy 2. Some hold that the prohibitions are entirely local and therefore carry no permanent universal application. Others argue that the provisions made by Paul are permanent and universally applicable because he appeals to the order of creation. On balance it seems to me that the former arguments are more cogent, if only for the fact that there are parts of this passage that are obviously not taken in a literal sense, that is, the statement regarding procreation and salvation of women. Therefore at the very least, caution is necessary before taking other parts of the passage too literally. But in regard to the appeal to creation, and if primogeniture was a valid argument, then we would have to say that all the living things created before Adam are superior to him!

Second, the concept of *helper suitable* for Adam (Gen 2:18) seems to suggest that Eve was created to help Adam. The argument here stands or falls on the basis of our understanding of the meaning of the word *helper,* which in general use is applied to a person who does not possess the qualifications of a technician. In a mechanic's workshop a helper is engaged not to repair vehicles but as an unqualified assistant takes care of the menial side of repairing machinery. This meaning of *helper* is often used to inform the meaning of the phrase "helper suitable for him." As a consequence, it is not uncommon to find marriage situations where the wife is little more than a glorified housekeeper who shares her husband's bed. But this is not the only meaning given for the word *helper.* We need to look to the Bible to see how else the word is used.

In several passages in Scripture, God is described as the one who helps Israel. We see this in 1 Chronicles 5:20 where God was a helper for the two and a half tribes who remained in the territory east of the Jordan River. In the Psalms, God is depicted as the helper of Israel in various contexts: in times of distress (Ps 20:2); when in danger from foes (Ps 54:4), and for general welfare and well-being (Ps 121:1-3). It would be preposterous to suggest that the Lord is an unqualified assistant brought along to help Israel to accomplish its tasks successfully. To the contrary, it is precisely because the help of the Lord is at hand that Israel is successful. It is this concept of help that should inform our understanding of the concept of helper used in Genesis 2:18.

Perhaps a couple of illustrations might clarify the issues here. In order to train my daughter to acquire the skills needed to ride a bicycle, I had to run behind her, sometimes holding the saddle to let her get on or off, to steady her when she appeared to be near to falling off and so on. In all ways I was my daughter's helper but not an unqualified assistant! Similarly, a midwife attending to an expectant mother in labor helps to bring a child into the world. The midwife's skills are vital to avert a catastrophe during childbirth. She is a helper but not an unqualified assistant. Men and women are equal and complementary in the task of fulfilling God's mandate to be stewards of the earth.

Third, the concept of headship in Ephesians 5:23, however it is understood, cannot mean a demeaning of women before men, even of a wife before her husband. To the contrary, headship is the privilege of responsibility so that the husband is charged like Christ to establish the conditions under which his wife and his children will grow into their fullest potential. That is the example of Christ who died for the church, his bride, long before it existed. Incidentally, this means that young men and women who aspire to marriage should be giving their lives for their prospective spouses. The challenge is to prepare adequately to make a good contribution to the relationship materially, emotionally and spiritually. Christ continues to make provision for the continued betterment of his bride, the church, until one day it will be perfect. The challenge of marriage, especially Christian marriage, is that our spouses should become better people as a result of having lived with us. This is what love means; this is what headship means. I find the context of the passage a much better guide for determining the meaning of the term *head* than the normal exegetical arguments based on word studies. One does not have to be a Greek scholar to appreciate the richness of the meaning of Christ's headship and therefore the example for every husband.

In addition, it is instructive that Jesus' attitude to women was revolutionary in his day. He treated them with unusual respect. He allowed women to be taught the word when it was customary only for men to be taught. He protected prostitutes without condoning their way of life. Relationships in general and marriage relationships in particular can and should be a window to the image of God in human beings. He has given us the example of love in the Trinity between the three members of the Godhead, and we are to follow suit. This leads naturally to a discussion of love.

Between stewardship and love—those two relational attributes of what it means to be made in the image of God—love, it seems to me, is the more significant as we seek to represent God here on earth. Love is not love unless it is given away. One cannot really talk about being a loving person in the abstract. There must always be a demonstration of love to another person or other people. This is true of God, who experiences true love within the Godhead, the Trinity: the Father, Son and Holy Spirit enjoy true love, leading in a truly remarkable way to harmony and unity of purpose. Human beings made in God's image must seek to demonstrate the same love evident within the Trinity.

Invariably when the Scriptures talk about God as love it is in connection with some tangible demonstration of that love (see Jn 3:16; Rom 5:8; 1 Jn 3:16). Unfortunately both the verb *to love* and the noun *love* are so much in use that they lack clear definition. Both words can mean so many different things and describe so many varied human emotions that this often leads to confusion. What does it mean to love? What is the evidence of love in our human relations? Where do we find clarity?

We turn for help initially to the language of the Greeks, which has at least four verbs to translate the one English verb *to love*. These are transliterated as *stergō, phileō, eraō* and *agapaō*. I will deal with them in this order because this is the natural or chronological order in which we experience love. A word of caution is in order here, however. This method of speaking about four loves goes back to 1960 and the publication of C. S. Lewis's *The Four Loves*. Recent studies have shown that whereas the four or five kinds of love are true to life, the link with each of the chosen Greek words is at best slender. The Bible, for instance, does not use *eros* in its texts in spite of speaking many times about sexual love.[50] This is a common weakness for word studies and the theologies based on them. So it is important that when dealing with biblical material the dictionary definitions of each word are not divorced from their original, biblical contexts. In the analysis that follows I will use the four loves paradigm because it fits the sociological and biblical examples I have chosen in this chapter.

Stergō means I feel affection for someone, especially "the mutual love of parents and children."[51] The word is uncommon and does not appear in the New Testament except in two adjectival forms: *astorgos* (at Rom 1:31 and 2 Tim 3:3; where the NIV translates them as "heartless" in Rom 1 and "without love" in 2 Tim 3) and *philostorgos* (Rom 12:10, translated "brotherly love"). *Astorgos* describes a person who lacks even the most basic kind of love, that is, the natural affection most people feel for those with whom they share common blood. *Philostorgos* describes the natural presence of filial feelings for one's common biological parents. In both contexts in these two passages, Paul is describing not just ungodly but unnatural behavior patterns. To lack basic human natural affection is inhuman indeed. C. E. B. Cranfield makes reference to the common practice in Paul's day of exposing unwanted babies to the elements, which would lead inevitably to their death and was in fact an act of infanticide.[52]

In our day *astorgos*, the lack of brotherly affection, has been clearly evident in high-profile cases of abuse of children that led to death. Since 2001 three shocking cases of child abuse have surfaced in the United Kingdom. The first was the discovery of the torso of an unnamed child who had obviously been killed in some form of ritual. The remains of his body had then callously been dumped in a river. Forensic examinations showed evidence of poisoning by the use of potent beans common to West African voodoo practice.

The second case of child abuse was the death of Victoria Climbié, a nine-year-old child whom a close relative had taken to England from her native Ivory Coast in West Africa. When Victoria died on February 25,

2000, her body was riddled with evidence of horrific maltreatment. Over a period of two years she had undergone every imaginable form of abuse, including sexual abuse and the failure of all the adults in the health care system, social services and the church to protect and save her from a terrible fate.

The third case, the murders of two ten-year-old friends at the hands of a school caretaker, rocked the public. The two girls were lured into the caretaker's house and were eventually killed by him. It was later revealed that he had a history of abusing children, and the British High Court sentenced him to life in prison.

In other parts of the world, restrictions on population growth, poverty, war and general callousness often lead to practices such as baby dumping, cavalier premature terminations of pregnancies, abuse of children, and child homelessness that leads either to begging or prostitution.

The enormity of this inhuman behavior stands in stark relief when viewed against two facts. First, a newborn baby is completely helpless. Without an adult to do everything for him or her, that child will surely die. It is precisely the vulnerability of the child, the complete helplessness of the newborn, and by comparison the omnicompetence of the mother or surrogate parent that create a bond incomparable to any other human experience. Second, the child is completely trusting, by virtue of his or her inadequacy and also by nature. That trust is rebuffed and repaid by abuse, which is true heartlessness, lacking in the most basic form of natural affections. To be human is to show natural affection, especially to those within the family.

African experience of family life and love is very rich. The establishment of a blood connection, however remote, often turns initial suspicion and even hostility into love and embrace. But even in this situation there is plenty of evidence of lack of affection. For example, abnormalities in children, including having new teeth appear first in the upper gum (Bemba, *ifinkula*), often led to the castigation of such a child as a bad omen, which was a death sentence. In bygone days twins would have suffered the same fate by virtue of being twins. But more common and contemporary is the harsh treatment stepchildren often receive at the hands of their stepparents. This is so endemic that it is evident even in the most loving, giving and outward-looking families within the church.

God has given us natural affections so that every child, and indeed every human being, might experience the warmth of acceptance and embrace within a small family unit. All human beings should count it a privilege to show love to every child, especially those born within the natural biological family.

Phileō shares with *stergō* the sense of filial affection, but it is broader, for this love is based on interpersonal associations between people. The word expresses the richness of associations covered by the word *friendship*. Friendships do not presuppose any previous bond; such "love" as may arise does so from the quality of the interaction. It is within the give and take of such relationships that a certain fondness, liking, admiration and respect emerge, which often become stronger than even some biological bonds. These friendships are formed in neighborhoods, schools, colleges, universities, workplaces and churches—wherever, in fact, people gather for extended periods of time sufficient for the bonds to form and blossom. Philadelphia, a compound form of *phileō*, and its masculine form are used in the New Testament to describe the relationship between fellow believers in Christ (see 1 Thess 4:9; Heb 13:1).[53]

Eraō and its noun form *eros* describe the often electrifying attraction between a lover and the loved one. The words describe passionate love, as for example within a marriage. *Eraō* and its cognates do not appear in the New Testament.

These three loves, *stergō*, *phileō* and *eraō* depend on the biological bond of parent and child, the give and take of friendships or indeed the erotic attraction between two lovers. This is what sets apart the fourth word *agapaō*, the verb from which we derive the noun *agapē*. The distinctions between the various words are not as rigid as the analysis suggests, but the overall implications are nevertheless valid.

Agapē requires no conditions. It is entirely dependent on the initiative of the subject, the lover. God invariably is the subject of this verb. He loves us because he wants to. There is no obligation on his part except his desire to love us, that is, to give himself for our good because he chooses to do so. His love in Jesus Christ is the fulfillment of his promise to Abraham that all the families of the world will be blessed, that is, will enter into the joy of knowing his love, forgiveness and friendship. These are the things that make for the flourishing of humanity. John 3:16 is a classic example of the use of this verb: "For God so loved [*ēgapēsen*] the world that he gave his one and only Son." It is for this reason that Jesus commands his disciples to love one another (Jn 13:34). He has set us the example in sacrificially dying for us, and he commands us to emulate his love for one another.

Although I have used these four words to discuss the various concepts of love, there is not, as indicated above, an assumption of a simple direct correspondence between the words and the concepts represented. Nor are there clearly defined boundaries between these words and the concepts behind them. But the fourfold definition does aid clarity and memory, and is therefore useful. All of us experience these forms of love throughout our lifetimes. It seems to me that *agapē* should be the basis of all our loving relationships. This is possible because we have experienced the free gifts of God in forgiveness and eternal life, and God commands us to love in this way. Such all-encompassing love will break the bounds of clannishness, tribalism, racism, superiority complexes and so on. It will reach out to every human being, thus making us all more and more what God intended us to be.

JESUS: THE IMAGE OF GOD

If human beings are made in the image of God, then Jesus *is* the image of God. Anything made in the image is not quite everything the original article is. But one who is the image contains the exact representation. To use an inadequate illustration: a photocopy, however good, can only be a second-class representation of the original. But a production from the original master plates at the printer reflects the originator's intentions fully. God is invisible (Col 1:15) and therefore not available for normal human investigation using the five senses: sight (except in the limited use of dreams and visions), smell, taste, touch and sound.[54] We have no way of knowing God unless he chooses to reveal himself in ways that make sense to us, and Jesus is the supreme method through which God is known. Jesus is said to be the exact representation of God; this theme runs like a thread through the New Testament. The apostle John says, "The Word became flesh. . . . No one has ever seen God, but God the One and Only, who is at the Father's side, has made him known" (Jn 1:14, 18).

In calling Jesus the Word of God, John uses the analogy of the normal human process that leads to one's expression of hidden thoughts. When a person wants to reveal what is hidden inside him, he "clothes" those thoughts with words, which are the symbols others pick up and translate, revealing what is in the originator's mind or indeed who the originator is. Jesus performs this function in relation to God. He is the embodiment or personification of God's thoughts—God's thoughts in human form. He is an agent as well as an integral part of God, or as John says, "the Word was God" (Jn 1:1).

This thought is reinforced by the apostle Paul, who claims that Jesus is not only the "image of the invisible God" but one in whom "all his [God's] fullness" dwells (Col 1:15, 19). This means in part that everything that goes into what God is—his Spirit, word, creativity, nature, power, redeeming love and so on—are to be found in total in Jesus Christ. So if we want to know who God is we turn to Christ, and in studying him and getting to know him personally we come into the realm of the knowledge of God. Jesus reveals God to us because in him is all the fullness of God.

Paul's words about Jesus, which capture perhaps the highest estimate of Christ's exalted position, are set in the context of the so-called Colossian heresy. Paul does not actually give us a definition of the false teaching in the body of the text, although careful exegetes have been able to cull from his positive counterarguments the basics of this subversive teaching.[55] The essence of the Colossian error may be captured in two questions. First, where is God and how can he be accessed? Second, what do people need to do in order to be fully prepared to present themselves before this God?

In answer to the first question, the teachers of this false teaching would say that God's fullness is to be found "distributed throughout a series of emanations from the divine, stretching from heaven to earth. These 'aeons' or offshoots of deity must be venerated and homage paid to them. . . . Christ is one of them, but only one among many."[56]

The second question relates to what we might generally call "salvation." How can a person be saved or adequately prepared to pass safely through the various stages on her way to the divine presence? The false teachers insisted on ritual observance of certain holy days and seasons, asceticism, self-denial and abstinence of all kinds, especially food and drink. Matter, in typical Hellenistic dualistic form, was associated with evil. Salvation was conceived of as the escape of the Logos or the pure spirit, currently trapped in evil matter, to reunite with the divine spirit.

In response to these aberrations, Paul effectively defines the place of Christ in the universe and in so doing paints a picture of what it means to be the image of God. He sets Christ out as the cosmic Lord who is the agent and author of creation as well as the origin of the church through his reconciling work, by shedding his blood on the cross. There is therefore no place for "elemental spirits" that must be placated through a system of works in order to win their favor. Jesus Christ bears the fullness of the Godhead in his material body. His imaging of God involves not only the inherent exaltation of a cosmic Lord, which he was before the incarnation and after the ascension, but also the process that began with "taking the very nature of a servant, being made in human likeness . . .

he humbled himself and became obedient to death, even death on a cross" (Phil 2:7-8).

Accordingly, D. J. Hall suggests that the "imaging of God" should not be conjured up purely on theistic grounds, that is, the exaltation of some human capacities, but on the basis especially of the sufferings of Christ.[57] The point he makes is valid and in keeping with the Reformers' thinking. He rejects the possibility that an ontological definition of the image of God is exhaustive and sufficient. But in making such a state-ment, it is important not to confuse two separate things: the process of sanctification, by which humans become more and more like God in character; and what it might mean to be created inherently in the image of God.

Perhaps a human explanation might help. Those who knew my late father see some resemblance between him and me. The likeness extends to physical appearance, speech mannerisms and certain other character-istics. In his day my father was not only a good husband; he was also a very good father. He was a community leader in both the trade unions and the church. In his latter years his health was plagued by high blood pressure and diabetes.

I think in general my father would be proud of me. Many of his values are reflected in my life, including family life, work and community lead-ership. There were things about my father that annoyed me, and you can imagine how horrified I get when I catch myself acting and reacting in those very ways (with an apparent inability to do otherwise)! I am to that extent a chip off the old block!

But suppose I had chosen a path in life that was totally self-centred, amoral or perhaps even evil, characteristics that would make my father turn in his grave. Would that diminish the fact of my being his child, my bearing the ontological marks of my paternity? Of course not! It is true to say that when my lifestyle more or less fulfills my father's ideological aspirations, I image him most fully. What we do as children of our par-ents is very important, but it does not *make* us children of our parents.

The Bible views the human being as made in the image of God. There is a clear distinction between humans and their biological relatives in creation. Again the Bible considers the human as a whole, "a unified activity of thinking, feeling, willing and acting."[58] People are neither disembodied souls nor soulless bodies. Humans are made in the image of God and more or less image God.

Some scholars emphasize a substantialist view of the image of God; others see a more relational definition. My view is that the truth combines both perspectives, and it is in that combination of views that we can catch a true glimpse of what humans were intended to be. Sin has made a big difference in our ability to image God. Some scholars argue that the image of God was lost with the Fall of Adam, and only in Jesus is there a possibility of that image being renewed or recreated. Sin is indeed a highly significant part of how the Bible views human beings, and I will look at it in some detail in the following chapter.

3

The Descent of Man

A FRIEND OF MINE WAS ABDUCTED AT GUNPOINT early one evening in the city of Lusaka, Zambia. His abductors took him in his car to a lonely place outside the city, where they beat him up, stripped him of all his clothes and possessions, and urinated on him, all the time threatening to shoot and kill him.

These were not idle threats. During that time many motorists had been shot dead in such incidents. Finally they left him in the dark. He was bruised, frightened, shocked and naked. He then had to walk more than three miles to the nearest police station to get help and report the ordeal.

Every pastor knows that even in the most respectable homes one finds untold suffering perpetrated by spouse against spouse, by parents against children and by children against parents. But suffering is not just at the personal level. The world is full of displaced people. I recall being horrified by the story of a dozen or so refugees who had trekked from Burundi through the Democratic Republic of Congo into Angola, finally making it to Mwinilunga in northwestern Zambia. The journey was long (like walking top to bottom through most of Western Europe) and dangerous, because Congo and Angola were experiencing terrible atrocities as a result of civil wars.

The refugees were running away from persecution and perhaps even certain death. Their only crime was that they belonged to the "wrong" tribe in their country of origin. In that group of refugees was a nine-year-old girl unrelated to any of the other people in the group. My second daughter had just turned nine when I heard the story, and I could not even begin to imagine what agony I would go through as that girl's father. In a similar group of refugees, a mother who was nursing a sick and dying child had to choose between burying her child half dead, so that she could keep up with her fleeing compatriots and provide for her own security, or lagging behind to nurse her child until what seemed to be an inevitable death, and so giving the poor unfortunate infant as decent a burial as circumstances allowed. This latter choice would almost certainly lead to her isolation and death.

Intertribal atrocities have plagued the two small countries of Burundi and Rwanda since 1959, culminating in the genocide of 1994, when nearly one million people were brutally executed in organized communal killings. The two tribes, the Hutus and the Tutsis, appear forever divided, and the bloodletting seems unending. There is much further evidence of evil in the world, of course; all one needs to do is turn on the news on any television or radio channel.

The really frightening thing about evil in the world, however, is that under the right conditions ordinary human beings can, and often do, turn into evil monsters. When one considers the numbers of people who died in the Rwanda genocide, is it unreasonable to assume that many ordinary, decent Christians were involved in at least encouraging the killing, if not actually killing other people? "How was it possible that the people we knew and loved could have been turned into the savages we saw night by night?" Meg Guillebaud's personal agony and anguish are almost palpable as she tries to come to terms with the worst African genocide affecting people she had grown up with, knew and loved.[1] John Stott, commenting on the reference to the heart in Mark 7:21, gives a helpful illustration of how nice people can become monsters:

The subconscious . . . what the Bible means by heart . . . is like a deep well with a thick deposit of mud at the bottom. Normally, being at the bottom, the mud is safely out of sight. But when the well-waters are stirred, especially by the winds of violent emotion, the evil-looking and evil-smelling filth breaks the surface—rage, spite, greed, lust, jealousy, malice, cruelty and revenge. These base passions keep bubbling up from the secret springs of the heart.[2]

SIN: A DEFINITION

From John Stott's words we can deduce that a definition of sin must contain two parts.

First, sin describes a condition intrinsic to the way human beings are—it is part of our very fabric. In this form it is not necessarily evident by sight, and normally for most people the condition does not lead into overt activities that can more easily be identified as sinful or immoral actions. But that does not mean they are not in this sense sinful. The psalmist uses the following words to describe the condition of sin in himself:

Surely I was sinful at birth,
  sinful from the time my mother conceived me. (Ps 51:5)

David wrote these words following deep conviction as a result of gross immoral conduct in which he not only violated Bathsheba's moral integrity by forcing her to commit adultery with him, but conspired to have Bathsheba's husband, Uriah, killed. In one series of events (2 Sam 11—12) David broke just about every one of the Ten Commandments. In acknowledging the gravity of his current sin, David looks back over his life to his conception and attributes even that to sin. Was this simply a theological statement, or did it have some personal reference apart from the Bathsheba episode?

We know from such passages as 1 Samuel 17:25, 1 Chronicles 19:1 that David was a stepbrother to his older siblings, for his sisters Zeruiah and Abigail were daughters of an Ammonite king, Nahash. It seems therefore that Nahash's widow—so far unnamed in the biblical records—married Jesse, and David was the result of that union. Is it possible that in referring to a "sinful conception" David is making reference to some improper conduct linked to the circumstances of his birth? There is no evidence in Scripture to suggest that this was so, and as far as we can deduce, his was a perfectly normal conception as the last of Jesse's sons (1 Sam 16:11).

David must be understood instead to be making perhaps the most profound statement about sin in the Old Testament. From the time of his conception, sin was a condition that permeated his entire existence. The presence of sin in his life went back to the earliest beginnings of his humanity, his conception. It is there from the start; it is latent and not only has great destructive potential but expresses itself especially in rebellion against God's word and will. The present calamity, his adulterous relationship with Bathsheba, is just a manifestation of what lies hidden in his human constitution. In fact, sin can be defined as "lack of conformity to the law of God in act, habit, attitude, outlook, disposition, motivation, and mode of existence."[3]

Second, sin is immoral or unethical activity that does not conform to the will of God. Mark's Gospel mentions "evil thoughts, sexual immorality, theft, murder, adultery, greed, malice, deceit, lewdness, envy, slander, arrogance and folly" (Mk 7:21-22). In this small section Jesus makes a distinction between those external activities that in his day were regarded as highly "sinful" and the internally motivated activities. The latter, on account of the fact that they have contact with the heart (indeed, they originate from the heart), are the really sinful things.

Mark's list is headed by "evil thoughts," which must be understood to be an overarching term covering the list that follows.[4] The "heart" in biblical usage was the seat of thought, will and emotions, representing the center of the inner self and therefore the locus of one's character. What comes out of the heart reflects a person's true character in a way that external activities do not. This is a difficult concept, for every external human activity, such as singing hymns in church or taking communion, must surely have a corresponding base within one's inner being. But the important thing is that external activities do not necessarily reflect what a person really is. Hypocrisy is the masterful ability of presenting an external set of activities, often in conformity with particular expectations, which nevertheless do not correspond to what a person really feels like inside.

Two general points emerge from these observations. The first is that if a person is to please God, then his or her heart must be in tune with the thoughts and will of God revealed in Jesus Christ. Second, there must be continuity between what we think and feel inside and what we say or do externally. Correct protocol for its own sake—giving the appearance of correctness outwardly—does not impress God. True Christian religion demands an alignment of outward act and inward thought. This is vital because the process of enculturation by which we are socialized into any community may well engender within us attitudes and characteristics at variance with the requirements of the Scriptures. Perhaps one of the best gifts a parent can give a child is the gift of transparency. True discipleship must align practice to the heart. Where variances arise, these then must be dealt with.

The list of twelve "evil thoughts" in Mark 7:21-22 has a remarkable resemblance to the second table of the Ten Commandments of Exodus 20, which may be intentional. Two comments on some of the words in the list will suffice.

- The first of the evil thoughts listed in Mark is sexual immorality. This vice includes not only overt acts of adultery and fornication but all manner of secret lust, as indicated by Jesus in Matthew 5:27.

- The final addition to the list is folly, used in the Old Testament wisdom literature to describe those whose attitude to God is wrong, which leads to poor attitudes not unlike those described as wicked (see Ps 14:1).

Lists of this kind were commonly used as a teaching tool and appear in several parts of Scripture, including Romans 1:24-31 and Galatians 5:19-21. At every turn of human existence and in whatever circumstance, traces and evidence of variations of the evil things the apostles list can be found. These are, however, only symptoms of the condition of sin within human beings.

THE ORIGINS OF SIN

The Bible helps us to understand the origin and nature of evil in human beings. It ascribes the origins of sin to the first human beings, Adam and Eve, who are consistently treated as historical on the same level as the patriarchs, Moses, David and all the others who fill the pages of biblical history. After God created Adam and Eve he put them in an environment, the Garden of Eden, where they were to serve a sort of probation. God gave them one command: not to eat of the fruit from the tree of the knowledge of good and evil (Gen 2:17). To be a moral human being includes the ability to distinguish between good and evil. It is plainly obvious, therefore, that God did not want Adam and Eve to remain unable to differentiate between good and evil. However, God wanted them to learn that lesson not by trial and error but by obedience to him, taking him at his word.

The tree of the knowledge of good and evil poses some problems. What kind of tree was it? Did it bear ordinary fruit such as apples or oranges? Quite likely, it did; the Bible does not say what kind of tree it was. Some suggest it was so named because anyone who ate of its fruit would have practical knowledge of good and evil. In effect, the tree was so named because of the prohibition God had given. The eating of the forbidden fruit, in an act of disobedience, would lead to a situation where human beings undertook to learn for themselves (in costly ways) the difference between good and evil. The tree physically offered human beings a choice between trusting God entirely or allowing other influences to have pre-eminence.

Many a parent will tell a child not to touch hot things, for they burn. Children will often obey, but the majority of us have scars that show our disobedience. Our parents would have saved us the pain and agony of touching red-hot things, but in our disobedience we did not believe them; hence the scars. The origins of sin in human history are similar. Adam and Eve, aided by the serpent (Satan in one of his many masquerades; see 2 Cor 11:2), went against God's command and ate of the fruit of the tree of the knowledge of good and evil (Gen 3:6). They had come to regard God's prohibition as an infringement on human freedom.

This has become very much an issue in this era of human rights. The assumed inalienable human right to free sexual choice, for instance, flies in the face of God's prescriptions for good relationships in matters of sex (see Ex 20:14). Today's human beings, like Adam and Eve, want to determine their own futures, elevating their rights over God. This is the essence of sin: seeking to live in opposition to, or independence from, God. Human beings and God can coexist harmoniously only when the former learn to live in total dependence on the latter.

The event in which sin first entered human experience is described in Genesis 3. The tempter, Satan (represented by the serpent), began by sowing seeds of doubt into the mind of Eve. "Did God really say, 'You must not eat from any tree in the garden'?" (Gen 3:1). Notice at once two things. First, there is a suggestion that God's word is "subject to our judgment."[5] The only sense in which God's word is subject to our judgment is one in which we seek to understand in order to obey, not in order to correct as if we were equal to God. Second, the serpent exaggerates the command of God in an attempt to show that God's word is not only unrealistic but unreasonable. Eve shows that she is hooked by her overcorrection; she says that the prohibition extends to touching the fruit (Gen 3:3). The tempter then follows this up with a categorical denial of God's word, "You will not surely die" (Gen 3:4). Further, the tempter boldly attacks the motives of God. He sets his word against that of God by saying that God's apparent love is in fact a smoke screen for envy, and that eating the fruit will reward Eve unimaginably! The trap is sprung, and Eve falls headlong into it.

This pattern of temptation is repeated in Jesus' temptations recorded in Matthew 4:1-11. It is important to realize that although this episode is popularly said to be Satan's "temptation of Jesus," the initiative was with God. The aim was to test Jesus, although Satan indeed did want to cause Jesus to sin. The clue to a better understanding of this passage lies in the three Old Testament quotations Jesus uses to overcome Satan's temptations. All three quotations come from the tests experienced by another "son of God," the nation of Israel (Hos 11:1) in the wilderness (see Deut 6:13, 16; 8:3). God tested the Israelites three times and at each turn they failed. The true Israelite, the true Son of God, succeeds where Israel had failed. God "drove" Jesus into the wilderness to be tested.

The first temptation aimed to divert Jesus' attention from doing the will of the Father to his own material needs. It was not wrong to turn stones into bread; what was wrong was to do so at the command of Satan and for Jesus' own comfort.

Satan then attempted to create an artificial crisis, thus asking Jesus to perform a feat that would "force" God's hand to save Jesus and prove to any doubters that he truly was the Messiah. But Jesus would not test God. His commitment was to live in total obedience to the will of his Father.

The third temptation involved the temptation to political glory—the same temptation that had faced the Israelites (Deut 6:10-15). Time and again the nation of Israel had succumbed to the temptation by renouncing exclusive loyalty to the Lord. Jesus dismissed Satan, refusing to compromise his obedience and loyalty to the Father for a hollow victory without the necessity of the cross.

Satan continues to tempt all human beings in these basic ways: causing us to doubt the word of God, appealing to our pride and promising us the world when in fact he is unable to deliver any of these things.

THE CONSEQUENCES OF SIN

Immediately upon succumbing to the temptation of the serpent, Adam and Eve experienced, for the first time, a demeaning sense of pollution and guilt. This experience drove a wedge between them and God, and they no longer wanted to be in his presence. When he came calling, they hid from him (Gen 3:8). This all-consuming sense of guilt and shame was followed by God's judgment, leading to pain and death.

The alienation from God, which started as a simple hiding away from his presence, has developed into a gulf between God and humanity (Is 59:2). Even in the wake of the Fall, human efforts at providing covering for their naked bodies were completely inadequate. It took God's kindness and the death of animals to provide Adam and Eve with clothes. Much later, the blood of Jesus Christ would prove the only effective cure and covering for human sinfulness.

THE UNIVERSAL SCOPE OF SIN

It is difficult to be categorical in setting boundaries within the sweep of history. Some feel that there are four basic sections: the first period includes all the books from Genesis to Samuel. The events center initially on creation, then the call of Abraham, but especially the exodus, followed by the conquest and settlement. In terms of leadership, Samuel brings to an end the epoch-making leadership of Moses and the judges, and introduces both the charismatic prophetic ministries as well as the institutionalized monarchy. Clearly apart from creation, the central feature of this section is the Moses story and the exodus.

The second period can be said to run from the monarchy to the end of the book of Malachi (end of the Old Testament). In terms of new revelation, it is the work of prophets like Elijah that introduce this new period. They are followed by all the writing prophets. It was during this period that the monarchy rose and disappeared; the northern kingdom snapped and vanished from the stage of world history, and the peoples of both Israel and Judah were sent into exile in Assyria and Babylon. The prophetic witness became a new form of revelation and sustained God's direct input into the lives of the people of Israel.

With the birth of Jesus we have a new form of revelation. It is accepted that revelation of God comes to its climax in Jesus' life, death and resurrection. In many ways what follows from the inception of the Jerusalem church in Acts 2 to the end of the book of Revelation is commentary on Jesus and his impact upon the earth. However, we do have a new and intensified activity of the Holy Spirit, which warrants the suggestion that this section can also be treated as a new epoch of revelation. Each epoch adds to the forward historical movement in God's involvement in human history.

For our purposes it is instructive to note that in spite of progressive revelation, sin is evident at every stage of history. The first human beings end their blissful relationship with God on account of sin in the Garden of Eden (Gen 3:6). After the flood of Genesis 7, as life was returning to some form of normality, Noah got drunk—with terrible consequences for his grandson Canaan (Gen 9:24). The book of Judges shows a clear cycle of disobedience, sin and suffering as a consequence of sin, followed by God's intervention (Judg 2:11-13, 17). During the days of the prophets, not only did Elijah challenge the false prophets of Baal, but all the other prophets (e.g., Isaiah, Amos) continually pointed out the sinfulness of the people, which eventually led to the exile in Babylon (Is 1:18; Amos 2:6-16). Even in Jesus' day corruption was rife, and in fact his arrest, trial and death reads like a catalog of miscarriages of justice, for that is what they were. Jesus died for sin (Mk 10:45; 2 Cor 5:21). The apostles soon had to deal with sin in the infant church. Peter challenged the deceitfulness of Ananias and his wife Sapphira (Acts 5:1-10). Jesus' last words to his church in the book of Revelation show that even then there were signs of sin within the church (Rev 2:14).

Paul speaks of the scope and nature of sin in his epistle to the Ephesians:

> As for you, you were dead in your transgressions and sins, in which you used to live when you followed the ways of this world and of the ruler of

the kingdom of the air, the spirit who is now at work in those who are disobedient. All of us also lived among them at one time, gratifying the cravings of our sinful nature and following its desires and thoughts. Like the rest, we were by nature objects of wrath. (Eph 2:1-3)

In these verses Paul captures something of the universality of sin. He makes the assertion that all humans have sinned (see also Rom 3:23). Adam, Paul would later argue, experienced sin and rebellion not just as a single person but in his representative capacity as the first human being. His experience of sin has since been transmitted in a "mysterious way" to all human beings.[6] Paul describes the human condition by using three expressions: *dead* (in your transgressions and sins), *following* (the spirit of disobedience) and *condemned* (to suffer the wrath of God).

The death Paul speaks of here is obviously not physical but *spiritual*. The Ephesian Christians were now alive both physically and spiritually but had previously been dead spiritually. Spiritual death is the separation that has occurred, on account of sin, between human beings and God their creator (Is 59:2). Human beings outside Christ can be likened to what in Bemba we call *infwa yenda* (death on two feet, or a walking corpse). A person has the appearance of being physically alive but in fact is so sick that it is just a matter of time before he passes into the next world. A recent similar phenomenon has appeared among people on steroid treatment for their human immunodeficiency virus (HIV) infection. As a result of their treatment, their bodies have developed to look like those of healthy weightlifters or professional wrestlers. Their bodies have the appearance of health, whereas unfortunately death hangs ominously over them.

Human beings can thus be divided into two groups: those who are alive to God and are therefore sensitive to his communication, and those who are dead—that is, not on God's spiritual wavelength and therefore unable to receive (let alone obey) his words. It is this condition of lack of responsiveness of the human heart to God that Paul calls "a state of death."[7]

Paul uses two keywords to describe the effects of spiritual deadness in human beings: *transgressions* (Greek *paraptōmasin*) and *sins* (Greek *hamartiais*). The former has the connotation of wilfully going against laid-down rules and is the essence of rebellion. In the story of Adam and Eve, God had expressly forbidden eating the fruit of the "tree of the knowledge of good and evil" (Gen 2:17). But with the help of the deceiver, Adam and Eve went against God's word (Gen 3:4-5). Transgression has therefore the meaning of committing sin by doing something forbidden, stepping over a boundary in defiance. It is a sin of commission.

The plural word *sins* (*harmatiais*) describes actions that fall below a prescribed standard (see Rom 3:23). Many of us know the experience of failing a test. In the Zambian educational system, passage from primary to secondary school is marked by an examination. Whether one passes or fails generally bears no relation to what is called the "cut-off" point. The cut-off point (always higher than the minimum passing grade) is determined on the basis of available secondary school places in any province. It does not matter that students passed the examinations and received a full certificate; if they fall below the cut-off point, then they cannot proceed to secondary school. They have fallen short of the standard. God has set standards of holiness and righteousness. Sin is a falling short of those standards. No one is exempt. All human beings fall short of God's standard.

In reality it is difficult to distinguish between transgressions and sins. An infringement of any of the Ten Commandments, for example, is at the same time a transgression (an act of rebellion) and a sin (a falling short of the mark) in that it reveals human disobedience and inability to keep the standards of God. But where do transgressions and sins stem from? In both cases the sinfulness stems from inner, evil motivation and bias.[8] I can illustrate this from my bitter personal experience of suffering from malaria.

The parasites that cause malaria are often injected into a person's bloodstream by a mosquito, and it takes about two weeks from the moment of infection for the various symptoms to develop and indicate that a person is infected. Normally, and for most people in Africa, treatment involves a course of twelve tablets of chloroquine and a few days of discomfort. Some parasites, however, live in the body tissue, such as the liver, and not in the bloodstream. Such parasites infect the bloodstream but retreat into the body tissue when the patient receives treatment. Normal treatment eradicates the parasites from the blood but not from the body tissue. There the parasites will bide their time until they multiply into sufficient numbers; then they will again infect the bloodstream. A more powerful drug is required to eradicate the parasites from the body.

Malaria symptoms (headaches, general body weakness, fever, hot and cold flashes, and so on) simply point to a more serious condition in the body. Similarly, transgressions and sins are merely expressions of a more deep-seated predisposition to do wrong; they are not the root cause themselves. The root is original sin, which "is the sinful state and condition in which every human being is born; actual sin, however, is the sins of act, word or thought that human beings commit."[9] Former Anglican Archbishop George Carey calls it "a wrong relationship with God which results in evil actions."[10] R. S. Anderson prefers the designation a "fundamental disorder."[11]

Another phrase pertinent to the discussion at this point is what is referred to as "total depravity." This phrase often causes offense; at face value these words can be construed to mean that human beings are so depraved as to be incapable of thinking, saying or doing anything good or beautiful. This is patently untrue. There are many examples of brilliant ingenuity, admirable creativity and wholesome works of prose, poetry and philanthropy. What the phrase "total depravity" means is that, however lofty our thoughts or wonderful our words or altruistic our actions, they are shot through with sin. Even humanity's "best acts and characteristics are subtly and deeply tainted with pride."[12] Although human actions and thoughts may be good, even brilliant in themselves, they are unacceptable as a basis for our acceptance with God. John Stott says, with characteristic candor, "When sin is stripped of all its disguises, and is seen in its ugly nakedness as the attempt to dethrone God and enthrone self, it is evident that we are incapable of doing anything to gain acceptance with God."[13]

Motivation is an all-important factor in this issue. The difference between bribe and gift lies in the motive behind the transaction. Even the exercise of writing on such a topic—exposing the sinfulness of human nature—is sometimes motivated by ideas of personal significance, grandeur, importance, power and influence. Dabney puts it this way, "The human conscience, the highest department of rationality, has its accuracy in decision making diminished by evil intent and desire."[14] To say that "human beings are sinners" (another offensive phrase) simply means that human will, originally created to be in harmony with God, is now in discord: "Your iniquities have separated you from your God" (Is 59:2). It is a statement of fact, not a politically incorrect moral judgment on the character of a particular individual. "It is that nothing we can do is perfect by God's standards."[15] Dabney makes the same point in these words:

> While there is something of true virtue in many secular acts and feelings of the unrenewed, which deserves the sincere approval and gratitude of fellowmen to them, as between man and man, there is in those same acts and feelings a fatal defect as to God, which places them on the wrong side of the moral dividing line. The defect is that they are not prompted by any moral regard for God's will requiring them. "God is not in all their thoughts."[16]

It is thus futile to work out a human religious system as a basis for either pleasing God or having a relationship with him. It just does not work. Anything we put our hands to will be rejected by God because it falls far short of his glory or standard of perfection (Rom 3:23). The only religion that pleases God, and is therefore acceptable to him, is one that has developed on the basis of his Word—that is, a religion he himself has revealed. Even then, the evolved system may not always remain true and faithful to his Word. There is a need for constant vigilance, analysis, evaluation and comparison based on the Word of God. By nature human beings are dead to God on account of the sin that is integral to their constitution.

The deadness in relation to God is compounded by being alive to the ruler of the power of the air (Eph 2:2). In his statement "You followed the ways of this world and of the ruler of the kingdom of the air," Paul uses the word *periepatēsate*, which is literally "you walked." People are often influenced by others or by ideologies. Such influences then determine how a person "walks" or lives. A person possessed by a spirit walks or lives according to the dictates of that spirit. The manner of life of the Gerasene demoniac was determined not by his humanity but by the legion of demons that possessed him (Mk 5:1-20). He walked according to the desires of the spirits that lived in him. In his lifestyle "there was no freedom, but rather a fearful bondage to forces over which he had no control."[17]

There are three ways in which the influence of the ruler of the kingdom of the air is exerted upon individual human beings. These are, first, conformity to the *ways of this world*, second, adherence to the *ways of the ruler of the world*, and third, the *cravings of our sinful nature*.

THE WAYS OF THIS WORLD

Paul warns us of the danger of conformity to "the pattern of this world" (Rom 12:2), using essentially the same phrase as is found in Ephesians 2:2. In Romans 12 Paul's command has the force of resistance to conformity, whereas in Ephesians 2 there is an acknowledgment that such conformity has already taken place. There are powerful forces that hinder the effective running of the Christian race. So what do we understand by conformity to the pattern of the world?

One of the answers lies in the process of human socialization, which ensures that we are conformed to that pattern of the world into which our parents are socialized. I do not here intend to give the impression that socialization in its entirety is evil, but it is one vehicle among many that is used to shape us into a worldly form in which we might gain attributes at variance to the will of God. Imagine two children born under exactly the same conditions, perhaps even delivered by the same midwife. In three years' time those children will exhibit very different characteristics. Taking into account their possible biological differences, they might speak different languages or exhibit different ways of speaking the same language. They might eat the same foods, yet prefer them prepared differently. The fact that they both are biologically human or were born in the same hospital at roughly the same time does not account for their differences. The processes of socialization to which they have been subjected have turned them into very different people. That is the natural process by which we become members of a particular society and so learn to invest greater or lesser value in certain attributes. Later on in life, peer pressure, education and encounter with other cultures may introduce into our lives new ways of this world.

Paul's use of the word *world* (*aiōna*) is not neutral. The word has definite connotations of an order at war with the will of God. Its antithesis is the righteous order of God. The ways of this world act like a prism, bending and distorting what passes through it, as in the following three examples.

1. *Tribalism.* Zambian children are taught through a natural process of socialization to value their tribes and hence their tribal identities. But what should be a natural and healthy pride in one's tribal or ethnic origins and identity often assumes an importance bordering on worship of the tribe. So strong is this feeling that, if need be, one is prepared to malign, maim and perhaps even kill in order to defend such an identity. Tribalism is a powerful form of racism.[18] The Rwanda genocide was basically a tribal conflict made worse by military and political ramifications.

At another level and for historical reasons, the Zambian church is divided along tribal lines. To be a Christian from the Kaonde tribe normally means one belongs to the evangelical church in Zambia, a denomination rooted in Kaonde territory and culture. The Baptists are largely Lamba, Brethren in Christ are Tonga, Presbyterians are Tumbuka and so on. The church in many circumstances becomes the guardian of tribal identity, the preserver of a tribal language that may be struggling against more aggressive tongues. True Christian fellowship across tribal boundaries is difficult if not impossible to attain. This undoubtedly is one of the major weaknesses of the African church today. Even in the bigger, multitribal denominations, the internal ecclesiastical power politics follow tribal patterns.

2. *Shame.* K. B. Maxwell says of the Bemba that

each Bemba person is so totally and thoroughly socialised that there is virtually no individual self-consciousness. Criteria of truth and value are socially, not internally generated and applied; responsibility is communal, not conscientious, and public shame, not guilty self, is the penalty for moral contravention.[19]

In a situation like this, terms like *repentance* and *confession* are often reinterpreted to mean something other than what the biblical writers intended. More often than not, repentance has come to mean no more than a public or private acknowledgment that one has been exposed. The real pain is the exposure to public shame and not the sorrow over the sin that has been committed. A case study may help to illustrate the point.

Chanda (not her real name) held a responsible position in her local church. She was pleasant, with a most generous spirit and considerable administrative skills. In her secular employment she was the purchasing manager for her firm. Besides being a leader in her local church, Chanda was also a leading member of the general synod of her denomination. Her disposition and training served her well in her varied tasks. She was a popular woman, admired by many. That was probably why news of her firing came as such a bombshell for her church community. The facts behind her being fired became common knowledge: manipulating the purchasing system of her employers in order to make herself lots of money while systematically destroying any incriminating evidence. The church community was not only shocked but terribly embarrassed.

On the Sunday following her dismissal, Chanda begged leave to address the congregation. She confessed her sins publicly and asked God and the congregation to forgive her. The congregation was pleased that she had seen the error of her ways; she had acknowledged her guilt, and they hoped that the process of restoration would begin. Several weeks later Chanda heard through the grapevine that her former employers had engaged court bailiffs to have all her personal effects confiscated in an effort to recover some of the loses they had incurred. Chanda stripped her house of anything she could take out and distributed them among friends and relatives for safekeeping. Later she used her ill-gotten gains to invest in a small trading company.

The church is not naive. It knows and expects that from time to time some of its members might fall from grace. But in such cases it expects repentance, confession and restitution. Chanda had blatantly lived a lie before being caught; afterward she continued to evade the course of justice and enjoy the benefits of her crimes. How can we understand her performance in the church the Sunday morning following her dismissal? What do we suppose she understood by the terms *confession* and *repentance?* Why did she not see the incongruity of continuing in office even after she had destroyed the trust vested in her?

In my view the answer lies in what I call the "good image syndrome." As a church leader, Chanda had been high on the ladder of public estimation. It was an image she had created and enjoyed. Her exposure to public shame and ridicule badly dented her public persona, her good image. Desperate measures were needed to repair the damage, including the willingness to stand in public and make a confession. The good image syndrome is a way of describing a Bemba cultural thought-form tied up with an excessive desire to be thought well of and thereby to remain prominent in the community—or at least in the eyes of an immediate interlocutor. Telling lies plays a big part in generating and sustaining such an image. In this example we see yet another way in which the Bemba "ways of this world" can and do distort the meaning of the word of God.

3. *Spiritism.* Spiritism is a significant factor in the socialization of Zambians (and no doubt many other sub-Saharan Africans). This area causes serious problems for the African church, for the world of the African is populated by spirit beings. While some are supposedly created as spirits, others (as mentioned earlier) are better referred to as the "living dead," or the spirits of ancestors recently departed this life.[20] These spirits participate in normal family life and are consulted in times of crises. J. S. Mbiti says:

> The living-dead are the best intermediaries between men and God. They know the needs of men, they have recently been here with men, and at the same time they have full access to the channels of communication with God directly or, according to some societies, indirectly through their forefathers.[21]

Growing up in Zambia, we are steeped in the spirit world. We witness libations being poured out on shrines and hear prayers offered to spirits of the ancestors for blessings and favor. But perhaps the most important factor is the area of witchcraft. We are conditioned to fear witchcraft and sorcerers. Strangely, neither education nor sophistication seems to have the power to eradicate or even minimize this fear. Church beliefs sometimes liberate people from it (although interestingly for Zambia the mainline churches have not been very successful in this regard; the breakaways and the African initiated churches have been singularly successful). Indeed one could say that this was the hallmark of membership in the Lumpa Church, one of the most successful churches in banishing witchcraft from among its members.[22]

Within the many mainline churches it is still common to find a leading member of a church who, when threatened with witchcraft, will immediately run to consult a diviner for protection. People known to have powerful *muti* (charms) are feared. They can easily take places on the leadership of any church. No one would dare to oppose them for fear of being bewitched. Ordinary members of the church will pay allegiance to Jesus Christ as Lord and at the same time maintain an active interest in traditional spiritual matters. Pentecostalism is gaining ground in Africa partly because it has the ability to demonstrate victory over traditional spirits and spiritual forces.

These are three of the ways of this world as they find expression in Zambian society. Every society will have its own characteristic exhibitions of the ways of this world and readers may want to consider what aspects of their own socialization have embedded certain cultural values and practices within their lives that run counter to the will of God revealed in Jesus Christ.

Paul warns us of the danger of following Satan, the ruler of the kingdom of the air. As an African, I have no difficulties believing in Satan as a personal spirit being (nor, incidentally, did the Lord Jesus Christ). Satan is an objective reality who influences people and always opposes the work of God.

The Bible is replete with references to the devil. Jesus acknowledges his existence (Lk 13:16; Jn 8:44), and Paul recognizes that there are evil spirit beings at work in the universe, with the devil ruling their evil realm (Eph 2:2; 4:8, 27; 6:11, 12).[23] Anyone who has witnessed spirit possession at close range will have no difficulty accepting not just the reality of a personal spirit called the devil but also the fact that his minions can and do inhabit human beings. He forces (or rather, enables) them to do inhuman or superhuman things. The devil is called the spirit of disobedience, for he energizes people to disobey God. Paul makes the claim that it is impossible in God's moral world to sit on the fence. One is indwelled either by the Spirit of holiness or by the prince of the kingdom of the air. We are urged to resist the devil (1 Pet 5:9) and to flee from every temptation he may throw at us (2 Tim 2:22).

The craving of our sinful nature can be rendered as the passions of our flesh. In my student days I learned an important lesson in regard to the cravings of the flesh. Two friends of mine and I went for a ten mile run. I had never done anything like it before but was sufficiently enthusiastic to follow my two friends. Everything went well until we got back. My colleagues, exhausted by the exercise, lay down on the grass to let their bodies cool down. All my senses, however, were filled with an overwhelming desire to replenish the body fluids lost while jogging, so I headed straight for the locker room, where I knew there was cold water to drink.

Water had never tasted as good as it did that afternoon; I drank and kept on drinking, until suddenly I felt faint. My legs felt wobbly and my sight grew dim. In panic I slumped on a bench in the locker room. One of my two friends found me in that condition and led me to my room, where I lay on my bed for almost one hour before I recovered. I learnt later that by drinking more water than I needed when my whole body was hot, I upset some balance in the body and nearly injured myself fatally.

It is all right to meet a need—a glass of water does indeed replenish diminished fluids in the body. But the timing of the attempt to meet that need is also important. Too little too late, or too much too soon, can be dangerous. I also learned that when a need becomes an appetite, it simply grows when it is fed. Feeding an appetite is not the same as meeting a need. There is satisfaction when a need has been met, but attempts to satisfy appetites always end in failure. An appetite grows with every attempt to feed it. If one wants to enjoy a really large meal, it is necessary to begin stretching the stomach walls several days or even weeks before the anticipated feast. But in such a gluttonous attempt to have "the meal that ends all meals," one may well do irreparable damage to the body.

When we turn desire to eat food into a love to eat food for its own sake, we are on the dangerous road to becoming gluttons. When we turn the normal and natural desire for sex into an appetite for sex for its own sake, we divorce sex from its rich environment of love, care, protection and true joy. We instead turn it into a commodity for sale. This leads to broken hearts and relationships, and gnaws at the very fabric of society, making us all the poorer in moral terms. What is true of food and sex is also true of drink, power, wealth, influence and pride. "These corporeal [bodily] appetites, being stimulated by the lusts of the soul, by a defiled memory and imagination, and by unbridled indulgence, become tyrannical and inordinate."[24]

Cravings of the flesh promise the ultimate experience but are deceitful promises (Eph 4:22). They never satisfy but lead instead to more and more cravings, until something gives way and we get hurt or we hurt other people. Satisfaction and happiness are illusory when sought for their own sake, and people who seek them in experiences are deluding themselves. A job well done may lead to satisfaction, but seeking satisfaction without the discipline to do the work well always leads instead to disillusionment. It is thus always folly to look for a job primarily thinking of the job satisfaction you hope to derive from it. Instead, you should resolve to do the job in hand to the best of your ability; the satisfaction will be thrown in.

Outside Christ, then, we are by nature in bondage to three very powerful and oppressive forces: the ways of this *world* into which we are socialized, the *ruler* (Satan) of the kingdom of the power of the air, and the cravings or passions of our sinful natures—*the flesh*. Traditionally theology has spoken of this unholy triad as the world, the flesh and the devil. It is important to emphasize, though, that we are not passively or unwillingly carried along these forces. It is precisely because we are susceptible by natural inclination or sin that we allow ourselves to be so enslaved. We are morally responsible, otherwise we could not be called to account by a holy God. But as it is we are guilty before God and are therefore objects of his wrath (Rom 1:18; 3:23; 6:23; Eph 2:3).

Associating God with anger often causes revulsion among both religious and secular people. In part this arises from our experience of human anger. Two real-world examples will suffice.

- A parent instructed his children to set off walking to a family outing. Sometime later he noticed that one of the children, probably distracted by something or other, had not obeyed the instruction. The father was so incensed by the apparent defiance of the child that he manhandled the child, and the child got hurt and eventually died from the incident. (This story, tragic as it is, demonstrates the petulant, irrational nature of human anger. Malicious intent, fear, desire for revenge or even careless action can stir it up completely arbitrarily.)
- Two brothers hacked their father to death because they suspected him to have caused the deaths of several relatives through witchcraft.

However much we might try to understand the outbursts that led to such fatalities, we cannot but feel revulsion toward this kind of anger. The Bible itself often condemns such outbursts of anger (Eph 4:31; Col 3:8; Tit 1:7), so naturally we are tempted to feel that such an emotion cannot or should not be part of God's character. Certainly many expressions of human anger contradict the nature and character of God, but what then is the origin of anger, and how should it be expressed?

It is a common fallacy to say that Christians should never get angry, for many things in the world should make everyone angry. Anger is a perfectly good human emotion. It is a gift of God and has an important role to play in human relations. Paul says clearly, "In your anger do not sin" (Eph 4:26); it is acceptable to be angry, but we must resist the temptation to sin in our anger. Anger is like red traffic lights: unless proper attention or caution is given to these warning signs, something will go terribly wrong. It is the proper management of anger that is the real issue. Two examples demonstrate what I mean by human management of anger for good: the first is taken from the world of athletics; the second from the arena of politics.

Carl Lewis is one of the world's best ever Olympic athletes. I recall watching him on television at the Seoul Olympics of 1988. He had just participated in and won an event, and the medal presentation followed.

Then he raced across the field to the long jump. He found to his obvious dismay that his name was on top of the list. He asked to be scheduled further down the list of participants so that he could catch his breath before attempting his first jump. The steward responsible, however, would not allow him to (probably the steward did not feel he had the authority to make the changes).

Lewis was incensed. A BBC commentator was heard to say that someone responsible ought to intervene quickly, before Lewis did something he might regret. Later Lewis was interviewed and asked about the incident. He replied that instead of taking out his anger on the steward (a normal human expression), he poured the energy the anger had unleashed into the longest jump he had ever made—and he won the gold medal! Here then is the key: anger unleashes energy; a bully uses that energy to hurt a victim; a coward employs the energy to aid the escape from danger; but this energy can be otherwise directed into constructive ways—for one's benefit, for the benefit of others, and toward the pursuit of peace.

The second example comes from Kenneth Kaunda's political career. Upon Zambia's independence, Kaunda was to become its first Republican president. In the days when Zambia was controlled by Great Britain and known as Northern Rhodesia, society was segregated along racial lines. In a butcher's shop, for example, black people were served through a dirty hatch at the back of the store, while white people were served through the front door. Kaunda went into one such shop through the front door and was immediately and unceremoniously ushered out. Although he was angry, instead of hitting back at the shopkeeper Kaunda vowed to work until no human being in Zambia could be treated like dirt on account of his or her racial identity. The energy released by that anger was a motivating influence for many to fight for racial equality.

Human anger is not all wrong. It may often be petulant and irrational with a strong tendency and potential for distortion, but that is due to the pervasive nature of sin and need not always be the preferred expression of human anger.

It is therefore also not necessary to shrink from the idea of the wrath of God, for even human beings demonstrate some of those same attitudes and characteristics of wrath found in God, especially in their attitudes toward death. When a death occurs, we bundle the corpse according to our varied traditions and consign it to the fire, the water or the earth. We who are alive remove death from our midst in much the same way that we get rid of dirt and other filth. Life and death cannot and do not coexist. Life, which is stronger than death, always removes death from its midst. This attitude toward death is settled and permanent.

God is spiritually alive, while we are spiritually dead on account of sin (Eph 2:1). In his holiness and righteousness God always reacts to sin in exactly the same way we react to death. He must get rid of sin and every vessel that contains it. Therefore, we who are sinful are by nature objects of God's wrath, a settled attitude arising out of his holiness and directed at anything that violates his standards of holiness and righteousness. "His anger is always a lawful reaction to the violation of a law or to opposition against his historically determined activity, in which he not only requites the violation or opposition, but also wills to effect the restoration of the order set between himself and man."[25]

A proper grasp of the Christian doctrine of sin and its effects in human beings is imperative if we are to begin to relate to God in a manner acceptable to him. In the words of E. R. Norman, human nature is "corrupted and partial, so that even in our most noble attempts at altruism we find ourselves constantly involved in moral ambiguity and flawed intention."[26] A misunderstanding of sin often leads to a superficial appreciation of the gravity of the human predicament, which leads in turn to ineffectual prescriptions. This is one of the major weaknesses of the "nurture" theory in the debate about the origins of sin—the theory that education, alleviation of poverty or the elimination of diseases can eradicate evil from the world. Proponents of this theory are surprised to find that the results of such reforms are simply developed cultured, educated, sophisticated, wealthy and healthy sinners. Sin, like the dreaded HIV virus, has the power to mutate and will find expression in any host, so long as that host is susceptible. And all humans, and the structures they create, are susceptible to sin.

God, whose holy law has been violated, is the only one who can prescribe the right remedy for the human predicament. "If God has made man for fellowship with himself, and if man has turned away and broken his relationship to God, then only God can forgive man and restore the fellowship."[27] This he has done in the death and resurrection of the Lord Jesus Christ. No other remedy is good enough because no other remedy can deal with sin.

Sin is part of the very fabric of what it means to be a human being. It is a condition of being human. To say that a person is a sinner may at one level point to this inherited condition or at another level point to a character showing evidence of sinful actions. The word *sinner* is not necessarily pejorative, nor is it judgmental, especially in the sense that it describes an integral part of the human condition. All human beings are born with, live in and die in sin. Sin has spiritual consequences and separates us from the possibility of a healthy relationship with God the Creator. Sin and sinners are subject to the wrath of God. The only remedy for sin is to be found in the sacrificial death of the Lord Jesus Christ. In chapter five I will return to the subject of the nature of the covenant of grace and the benefits for human beings of the death of Jesus Christ, but in the next chapter I will explore the subject of the human condition from a peculiarly African (Zambian or, more specifically, Bemba) perspective.

4

A Traditional African Anthropology

IN CHAPTER ONE I GAVE AN EXTENDED TREATMENT of the concept of *ubuntu* as an African vision of human nature. In this chapter I want to give one African's views of human nature. If you like, chapter one contained a macroview of human nature; here I am concerned to give a personal microview.

I have been unable to find reference to the image of God in human beings in any of the traditional Zambian or African understandings of what it means to be human.[1] This may be indicative of the limitations of my research, for the language of imagery in the African languages I am familiar with is limited to physical and immaterial likeness between generations. A son may be said to be the image of his father or a daughter the image of her mother or grandmother, but this language is never applied to the relationship of people with God, except of course in the appropriate translations of the Word of God into the many African languages.

In African anthropology it is impossible to deal with human beings apart from their cultural surroundings and identity. The society-based existence is evident everywhere—our predisposition is not "I think (or doubt or buy), therefore I am" but "We are, therefore I am." Africans find it difficult to conceive of a solitary or highly individualistic or isolationist existence. "I am because we are" is a very African attitude to life.

Culture therefore is the best milieu for understanding human beings in most sub-Saharan African contexts. Culture is dynamic; it constantly changes and adapts to new influences and challenges. In recognition of this fact, anthropologists no longer regard human beings from purely essentialist or ontological perspectives but relationally and dynamically. I begin with three stories to highlight the link between behavior patterns and the values they reflect.

In an interview on prime-time Zambian television, a bright Zambian female legal practitioner made the startling statement that all Zambian men are essentially adulterers! Adultery is a common indiscretion or sin in the world today, as indeed it has been from time immemorial. Zambians are probably no more or less adulterous than other peoples in this day and age; the woman's statement was based both on her experience in litigation in marriage cases and, more important, on her own personal (perhaps bitter) experience in marriage.

The topic being discussed was *polygamy*. Zambian law recognizes two basic forms of marriage: those entered into under customary law and those contracted under "the Ordinance." Those married under the Ordinance incur the wrath of the law if they marry someone else while still married to the first spouse, but those who marry under customary provisions are entitled to polygamy if the culture of the families involved allows it.

These two separate systems have their own appropriate enforcement agencies. The magistrates' courts settle grievances arising from marriage under the Ordinance; other grievances are settled in customary courts superintended by local court judges—men and women chosen for their proven wisdom and knowledge of local customs. The two systems are incompatible, and trained lawyers are barred by their profession from participating in the proceedings of local courts.

The interviewee's own marriage had been solemnized under the Ordinance. Her husband was also a lawyer, in fact one of the country's leading legal practitioners who had at one time held a cabinet post as minister of legal affairs in government. They had been married for almost twenty years. During most of that time he had maintained another marriage, entered into on the basis of tradition, and had children with the other wife. He had not broken the law: the second "wife" was not recognized as such by the system under which he had married his first wife. though she might have some rights as a common-law wife.

Why had the interviewee not divorced her husband? She could certainly prove a case of adultery, which is accepted as grounds for divorce. She retorted that the exercise would be futile because all Zambian men were the same. In sexual matters they are not satisfied with one partner.[2] The next man she would meet and marry would behave in exactly the same manner that characterized her present husband (notice the underlying assumption of the necessity for remarriage).

In another situation Jamie, a development worker from the West, sought to befriend ordinary Zambian men, assuming that this would be useful for his own work as well as his social life. He joined a social club and mixed well, sitting, chatting and drinking with them. After several years of these encounters he concluded that "all Zambian men are adulterers and thieves," basing his conclusion on the topics that had dominated the men's conversations: infidelity in marriage and how to avoid paying back loans.

Further, a college bursar in the West, partly to justify himself and partly to explain why he had not bothered to check the facts before wrongly accusing a black African student of soliciting for donations under false pretenses, was heard to say, "When it comes to money we do not trust black African students." This is reminiscent of a comment by B. J. van der Walt, who said that the "Westerner tends to place too high a premium on such qualities as honesty, openness, integrity, perseverance, and so on. (For that reason the Westerner will often consider the African dishonest, and the African will consider the Westerner impolite)."[3]

One could easily dismiss these stories as either sexist or racist. But perhaps the right attitude is to ask what truth the generalizations may contain. What does that truth reveal about an adequate understanding of who I am as an African? What values are important to me, and how will these values, rightly understood, help us in communicating the timeless truths of the gospel into the ever-changing social world of the African?

DEEP AND SURFACE CULTURES

The imagery of an onion, with its layers of skin, can help to visualize the complex cultural makeup of any human being. At the center we can expect to find one's religious convictions and the essential elements of one's vision of life—the way one views oneself, the world and one's place in it—as well as values and norms that characterize one's worldview. The remaining circles encompass material and spiritual creations such as marriage, initiation rites, work, family, healing, the church, the laws of the state, customs, behavior and habits. What is in the first circle—what we might call the inner person—is not visible but completely permeates and regulates what is said and done in all the other circles. The "inner, deeper cultural layers determine and direct the outward layers." Whereas the latter is clearly discernible and thus easier to describe,[4] for it is clearly discernible, the inner core, the vision of life, is more difficult to identify and describe.

There are other ways of presenting this same reality. We may borrow biblical metaphors such as trees (underground roots support and feed the stem, branches, leaves and fruit above ground) and buildings (an underground foundation supports a visible superstructure). Harold Turner has developed another helpful metaphor, that of surface and deep levels of cultures.[5] The surface, expressive or visible cultures relate to personal and public forms within our social existence. Some of these forms are highly localized, while others are widespread, national. This is particularly so for a country like Zambia and no doubt many others created by decree on a drawing board by imperial colonists. The boundaries drawn often cut through whole ethnic groups, consigning them to different countries. For example, the Chokwe people now live in Zambia, Congo and Angola! Other similarly divided groups include the Ndebele of Zimbabwe and South Africa, the Ndau of Zimbabwe and Mozambique, and the Tumbuka of Zambia and Malawi. The national cultures in these countries hardly exist. Those that do are inventions that bear the hallmarks of the cultural forms of the colonial masters.

Some of these personal forms will relate to the way people live, including their dress codes and personal appearance, the kind of architecture and furnishings that characterize the majority dwellings, the manner in which food is prepared and eaten, and indeed what kind of food is eaten. This will also include what people do to entertain themselves and their guests, the music they create and listen to or dance to, the manner in which they dance or sing, what kinds of guests they entertain, and how these are chosen. Other forms of expressive culture will include the nature of greetings—whether people prostrate themselves, kneel, shake hands, clap their hands, bow and hug or kiss each other.

Funerals are of particular interest. In my culture, when a person dies the members of the extended family invariably drop all but the most essential of duties and gather at the funeral home for several days and nights, until the deceased is buried. During the time before the burial we meet many relatives. A lot of them will have traveled long distances to get to the funeral. We mourn the dead and comfort the bereaved, we catch up on family news and increase the extended family networks, and we consolidate the family solidarity we so treasure. I did not really understand how significant these rituals are to me until I had to cope with the death of a close relative while living in self imposed exile with no way of attending the funeral. I have been left with a sense of incomplete closure and some very raw feelings.

We also include under this category of surface culture the way people mark rites of passage, including who has the right to know when a pregnancy has occurred, who names the child, what is the source of the name and how the child relates to grownups. Relations between one generation and the next are always formal, but relations between alternate generations are free and easy. A young child can address a grandparent as if they were equals! The functions and responsibilities of the biological father in relation to the child will be defined by culture. In my culture traditionally it is the child's "male mother" or mother's brother who is more significant than the biological father. He is the person responsible for discipline and often the material support of the child. The expressive culture will be even more evident in the way marriages are conducted. A young Zambian man may decide to marry a young woman, but the process includes the appointment of a go-between to break the news to the girl's family and to negotiate terms for payment of dowry or *lobola*.

WHEN TWO CULTURES MEET

We observe a complication in surface cultures when a major transition takes place, as has happened at the interface between the gospel and local cultures or indeed between Western and local cultures. Some of the results are bewildering, while others are humorous.

I had been brought up to respect my superiors and betters. One of the ways to do this was to avoid eye contact at all times, especially when receiving instructions or being rebuked for misconduct. This worked well at home and all through primary education, where all the principal players were Zambian. In my first year at secondary school, at the age of fourteen, half the class was black Zambian and the other half consisted mainly of white boys, most of whose parents came from all over the world. The teachers were all white. One day I misbehaved; Mr. O'Hagan was not at all pleased and began to give me a dressing down. As a good African boy I looked down to show my respect for him and hopefully to convey my sense of remorse and contrition. Mr. O'Hagan was furious and demanded that I look into his face, a thing I could not physically do!

The deaths of "my father" were also a source of constant confusion.

All my father's brothers and cousins are fathers to me. I would never address them by any other title or name but "father." The first time a student asked for time off to go to a father's funeral, there was a lot of sympathy all around. But when it happened again and again, all sorts of conclusions were drawn by our teachers—they thought we were inveterate liars who assumed they were all dim!

More serious is the matter of names. Bemba-speaking people of northeastern Zambia are somewhat peculiar in that we do not traditionally have surnames. Other ethnic groups in the country do indeed have clan names or surnames, which all the males bear;[6] we always receive the "belly-button" name at birth (or perhaps when the remnant of the umbilical cord drops), which is usually the name by which a person is distinguished. If the same name is common in the village, then the distinction will be made with reference to one's parents or grandparents. The first major name change will occur when one's firstborn arrives. The "belly-button" name falls out of use and may only be used by one's very close friends or relatives. In its place a person is called the "father of . . ." A similar name change will occur when grandchildren are born. My father's "belly-button" name was Mutale. When he went to a mission school, he needed to have a Christian name and surname. Since he already had an African name, it was only necessary to choose a name from the Bible or some other English name. At his baptism he became Joseph Mutale. All his brothers went through the same process, and the result was that all four of them had different surnames to their dying day.

By the late fifties when I started school, the concept of surnames was understood to be necessary—though not in the Western manner of understanding. I was always referred to as Kapolyo, son of Joseph, or more simply Kapolyo Joseph. When I went to secondary school my English headmaster decided to correct the "mistake" of my African name coming before my "Christian" name, so from then on I have been called Joseph Kapolyo. My older brother has a different surname from me, as do all my other brothers.

What happened to names also happened in relation to houses, marriage ceremonies, music and so on. Indeed expressive or surface cultures change quite easily. I started life in a little house of mud, poles and a thatch roof with no electricity or running water. Now I live in a medium-sized red brick house with most modern amenities. Similarly, I look after my own children and play only a supporting role to the offspring of my sisters, and only if asked.

Changes are harder in the core or foundational culture, however. Like the foundation of a house or the roots of a tree, this basic aspect of culture is not readily visible.

> It is a complex for which we use many different descriptive terms—a complex of axiomatic, unconsciously assumed convictions, belief systems, values, mind-sets, stances, reference points, frameworks, paradigms, and so on. These form the ultimate creative and motivating forces and controlling factors operating at the expressive or surface levels, whether in parent or sub-cultures.[7]

This is the illusive, inner, deeper, foundational culture that forms the core in which resides a people's vision of life, the home of their worldviews. Most ethnographic descriptions of culture deal at the surface level, although studies of myth and ritual have led the way into a deeper understanding of what lies below the surface.

At coffee time this morning a veteran missionary and indefatigable world traveler was giving advice to a colleague about visiting Korea for the first time. One piece of advice was never to drink water in public while facing the audience or congregation. This, it seems to me, illustrates the superficial nature of most of our attempts to teach intercultural studies to those about to cross cultural boundaries with the gospel. We all too often tell them to avoid making mistakes at the surface level. It is indeed important not to drink water in public while facing the crowd or to blow one's nose in public even if one has a handkerchief, or hand over items with one's left hand and so on. But these are hardly the issue if we are going to affect people deeply with the gospel of Christ. It may well be that the "conversion" of deep culture is something that only the natives can bring about with the help of the Spirit of God as he leads them in discovering God's will through his Word.

SOME CORE OR FOUNDATIONAL CULTURAL VALUES OF THE BEMBA

Here are some of the values that belong to the core, the foundational culture, that constitute a vision of life for the African Bemba.

1. Religion and spirituality. The first is what we may call *religion.* This term is probably misapplied to sub-Saharan Africans. There are Bemba words for "praising God" (*ukulumbanya Lesa*), "serving God" (*ukubombela Lesa*) and "thanking God" (*ukutotela Lesa*), but the Bemba people do not have a word for religion in their vocabulary.

J. S. Mbiti is perhaps the first African to attempt a thorough systematization of what in my view is erroneously called "African religions." Mbiti himself admits this much in saying that this is not an easy task. For "Africans are notoriously religious. . . . Religion permeates into all the departments of life so fully that it is not easy or possible always to isolate it."[8] But he proceeds to nevertheless treat "religion" as if it were a separate category from other entities in life, a category that can be systematized. This was his first mistake, for there is no body of orthodoxy preserved either orally or in literary form in the so-called African religions. The one thousand or so African ethnic groups (tribes) do not share a monolithic system of religion. Instead they have different beliefs expressed variously depending on need.

This is not to say that some beliefs and practices are not widespread, or that they do not bear any resemblance to expressions of spirituality found elsewhere in the world. Migrations, similarity in kinship systems, wars, famines, witchcraft eradication movements and intertribal trade all combined to insure crossfertilization of ideas and practices. In this regard J. V. Taylor is right in suggesting that "we may reasonably claim that we are dealing with the universal, basic elements of man's understanding of God and of the world."[9] But this recognition does not amount to a promulgation of a religious system, which can be systematized around the theme, for example, of the African concept of time.

Mbiti, along with many other Africanists, is also wrong in calling the collection of "traditional beliefs, attitudes and practices" of African peoples a religion. The isolation of beliefs in deities and the whole spiritual side of human existence is a Cartesian creation imposed on a description of African experiences. The Enlightenment demands classification, but life for the African must be embraced in its totality. Rationalism demands that life be broken up and classified in order to be labeled and thereby, presumably, better understood. Classification in itself is not a bad thing—it depends on what one does with what is so classified. In modernity, classification almost invariably leads to the process of the privileging of human minds over everything else; spiritual practices are therefore classified in the category of religion, which is then deemed a private pursuit that belongs to the area of personal subjective opinion. It is divorced from ordinary life in the public domain. African practice until the onset of Christianity knew no such classification.

In fact, one of the major weaknesses of Christianity in sub-Saharan Africa, as I will seek to demonstrate in this chapter, is precisely because it is a religion, "a classroom religion" for that matter.[10] It therefore fits not into the inner person—the deep culture that is the locus of the vision of life—where it naturally belongs, but rather (and unfortunately so) into the second set of concentric circles in our proverbial onion, or the expressive culture in the area of material and spiritual creations. It is thus not an integrating element in life. For this reason it is more accurate to speak not of African religions but African spirituality, a living faith.

Spirituality, unlike popular types of religion, is an integrating principle of life and does have those qualities of control and powerful influence over life in its totality. If this understanding and practice of spirituality in Africa had been transferred to the practice of Christianity, the church would be healthier, would be authentically African and would exert greater impact on life in its totality—personal *and* public. As it is, African spirituality controls and certainly permeates the practice of Christianity. "Christianity thus seemed like an ideal which people wanted to aspire to, but practically they continued living according to the normative system of their ethnic groups."[11] Van der Walt states that "Westernisation has not touched their essential being."[12]

Traditional Africans do not maintain a dichotomy between spiritual and secular values. "No distinction can be made between sacred and secular, between natural and supernatural, for Nature and the Unseen are inseparably involved in one another in a total community."[13] Many Africans understand that the material world is firmly connected to the spiritual world, and spirituality is the tie that binds human beings to the world of the ancestral spirits and gods. The practices of many African peoples show that they strongly believe in God and in the spiritual world.[14] An illness, for instance, is never even considered—let alone treated—in isolation. Contrary to normal biomedical practice, an illness is treated as part of the person suffering within the context of the community, which includes both the people alive and the spirits of the ancestors.

I experienced this as a child when I received treatment for the many abdominal ailments that plagued me. My maternal grandfather would take me to a bush he knew to have medicinal qualities for dealing with abdominal disorders. He would instruct me to put my hands behind my back, to close my eyes and to walk toward the bush. Upon reaching the low-lying leaves I was to bite off a leaf at a time and chew it, swallowing the sap and spitting out the rest. While I was walking he would walk alongside, saying prayers to God through the spirits of the ancestors. That is why the Bemba say, *ukwimba akati: kusanshyuku nu Lesu* (to dig a small stick, you add God), meaning that to be successful at finding the right roots for medicinal application one needs more that just knowledge of the relevant bushes—one needs the efficacious presence of God and the good will of the spirits of the ancestors in digging up the roots or presenting the sacrifices, as well as in applying the medicine. What was true of treating bodily disorders was also true of endeavors like hunting, preparing gardens for planting and going on long journeys, and deprivations like lack of food in times of drought.[15]

Spiritual activities. The second core value, which derives from the first, is the growth of varieties of *spiritual* activities such as rain making, healing, witch finding and sorcery (more widely referred to as *witchcraft*, a term Mbiti disparages and desires not to be used at all).[16]

Africans are very spiritual. Unlike their Western counterparts, they have no need to be convinced of the existence of God. Many are even monotheistic. Both the humanist rationalism that characterizes the West and the atheistic materialism that sums up communism are foreign to the African mind. A tiny group of diehard men and women swallowed the Marxist doctrines during the Cold War era, yet even they must have a tough time at funerals. (I suspect that at those times they conveniently ignore their philosophies.)

I recall standing at a graveside conducting a committal for an elder in a church who had died tragically in a road traffic accident. At the appointed time I invited the family and friends to follow me in throwing into the grave a token amount of soil. Many responded, including the younger brother of the deceased. In his remarks he promised the dead brother (or perhaps the spirit of the deceased) that within twelve months the person responsible for his death would similarly die. The promise was a commitment, first, to seek a diviner to discern the person responsible for the death,[17] and second, to use magic or witchcraft to cause the death of that person. Such countermeasures are common both for protection and for offensive use of magic. Many if not most African peoples believe that lots of human beings have power to tap into the supernatural realm and use such power mysteriously for harm or good. Many Christians of good standing are intimidated by threats of witchcraft.

It is a fact that a number of people on death row at the Zambian maximum security prison are men who caused the death of another at a funeral. In northwestern Zambia it is believed that on the way to the grave, a spirit will take hold of the bier, bind the pall bearers and the coffin, and lead them to the person who has caused the death. The power of the spirit, which at that point cannot be resisted, not only seeks out the "culprit" who caused the death of the deceased but uses the coffin as a ram to batter the culprit to death!

In spite of these horror stories arising from African openness to the spirit world, it is precisely this openness to spiritual things that has made it easier to account for, and is in part responsible for, the phenomenal growth of the church in the developing world. The important question is, which spirit is one in tune with?

Commitment to the group. One of the hallmarks of Western Christianity from the time of the Reformation and the Industrial Revolution is the concept of "faith as a matter of individual decision and individual application,"[18] what John Taylor calls the "isolated man with his intensely private world."[19] On the contrary, for the African person such isolationism is unimaginable. Taylor is so captivated by the all-embracing presence of the group that his chapter on an African anthropology titled "What is Man?" is simply a description of an African person's incorporation into and existence within the extended family:

> The sense of the personal totality of all being, and of a humanity which embraces the living, the dead and the divinities, fills the background of the primal world-view. But the foreground in which this solidarity becomes sharply defined and directly experienced is the life of the extended family, the clan, and the tribe. This is the context in which an African learns to say I am because I participate. To him the individual is an abstraction; Man is a family.[20]

My nuclear family—that is, the immediate family to which I belong as a son—at the moment comprises sixty-eight people (three have died: my father, one niece and a nephew). There are four generations included: my mother (parent), twelve of us (children) plus all our spouses, all our children (grandchildren), and three great-grandchildren. My extended family comprises the nuclear families of my parents' siblings and numbers in excess of two hundred people. But that is not all, for all my father's and mother's collateral relations and their families are also members of my extended family. If we were to count them all, there would be no fewer than five hundred. This is what is called in Bemba *ulupwa*—one's paternal and maternal relatives.[21]

Legally defined, a family is "a socially recognised union of two people and any offspring from that union."[22] This is what the Bemba would call "those of one house"; that is, they have one mother and one father. Culturally and practically this is the least significant of the definitions of *family*. It corresponds to a household, although even a household would normally be greater in that it includes all the people who live together and share the same dwellings, food and other basic essentials.

Ulupwa among the Bemba corresponds more to the kinship group, and that really only to the maternal relatives (this is especially so because the Bemba are matrilineal), but in practice bilateralism is common. Two proverbs illustrate this: (1) *abana ba mfubu: bangala amatenga yonse* (children of a hippo play in all the pools of water in the river or lake), which means that children belong to both their paternal and maternal kin; (2) *umutembo: ufinina konse* (a heavy burden weighs heavily on both sides), which means the duty and cost of bringing up children must be shared equally between the two sides of the family. Both sides of the family should recognize their obligations to the child as a member of the two families.

The extended family combines all the benefits of a full-fledged social security system without any bewildering red tape. "The family is a refuge in both the urban and rural areas, and the only institution providing some form of social security."[23] Children needing school fees appeal to the family members, who will invariably oblige. Children needing to be housed for any number of reasons will find a home in the house of a member of the family. Elderly people, parents or uncles and aunts who need to be looked after will not normally be shunted off to an old people's home but will be cared for by their own children at home. The system is flexible, efficient and user friendly.

The sense of solidarity of the family is a felt thing. Nowhere is this more real than at a family funeral, where the physical presence of all relatives is imperative. Sometimes the necessity arises from fear—a person's absence could be interpreted as evidence that they are the source of witchcraft that led to the death—but in general it is the duty of relatives to attend all funerals. At the funeral house itself, the sheer number of relatives makes the burden of grief light. Physical duties like baby care, cooking, cleaning and doing laundry are all done by the many gathered willing helpers. Babies become the focus of particular attention as they are introduced and passed around to relatives they have never seen. The prosperous members of the family make contributions to pay for the gathering and the funeral expenses. The camaraderie is also very significant: family stories are told, and family histories may be recited for the benefit of the young. Identity crisis is not really a problem on the African continent, although it may be so among the African diaspora in the impersonal cities of Europe, America and elsewhere.

There are difficulties with the extended family system. Some unscrupulous people can easily abuse it—lazy people can opt out of their obligations and instead move from one relative's house to another in search of a more comfortable life—but abuses do not outweigh the benefits of the system. There are, however, some important issues in relation to the church, including fellowship, support for the church, hospitality, individuality (personal and in relation to any given marriage) and priority of relatives. Let me deal with just two of these: fellowship and priority of relatives.

Christian fellowship and the African extended family system. Fellowship is an essential part of what it means to be Christian. The apostle John considers it to be the grounds for the incarnation (1 Jn 1:3-7): Jesus came into the world that he might create the basis for fellowship. The word *fellowship,* from the Greek *koinōnia,* is used in the New Testament to describe the church in terms of community, participation and, of course, fellowship. At the basis of the use of this word group is the idea of a common and shared background. In the Christian sense this stems from our "being united in Christ . . . participation in the Spirit" (Phil 2:1). The Christian heritage includes primarily a participation in the life of the Father, the Son and the Holy Spirit. These things cannot be changed because they are bestowed on us by God.

I have a brother who has lived for the past quarter of a century in North America. He now speaks with an accent reflecting his chosen country, and his complexion is quite different from mine. We rarely correspond as brothers should. But there is nothing that either my brother or I could do to take away the fact that we will remain, in name anyway, brothers to our dying day. The sooner we start behaving as brothers in reality, the better for both of us. Similarly, Christian fellowship is not just what we share in common; it must issue in community of goods (Acts 2:43-47) and the giving and receiving of hospitality (Acts 9:43). These attributes find much common ground with the African extended family.

All who belong to any extended family share a common biological ancestry. Their blood, their names and to a large extent their culture can all be traced back to a common ancestor or set of ancestors. The extended family gives us identity and a strong sense of family or clan solidarity. The relationships between members result not only in words of affirmation but especially in deeds of solidarity, including many of the attributes of a fully functioning social security system in the West. But more than that, there is a strong personal social support structure to meet the needs of the members at all times.

One would have assumed that the similarities in attributes between the African extended family and the church would make it easier for the African church to live out the concept of fellowship more fully. But sadly, in many places the experience of fellowship in the natural family is so real and exclusive that it hinders and discourages fellowship in the church. The sense of solidarity stemming from common ancestry is so strong that it acts as a barrier to the idea of extending the same sense of community to total strangers. Tribal churches thrive on this weakness.

"Priority of relatives" is the term I use to describe the fact that in personal, social and public life, relatives assume a place of priority over all others. In public life nepotism is a blight on the political and social landscape of the African continent. Priority of relatives distorts a proper sense of justice and fair play. But it is also and maybe especially so in marriage, where this priority of relatives can have a devastating effect on personal relations and on the ability of culture to negate the teaching of Scripture. The Bemba say, *umwanakashi: mwina fyalo* (a woman [wife] is always a foreigner), which means a wife must never be allowed to supersede blood relatives in a husband's priority. The woman, on the other hand, will never allow her sisters-in-law to assume a place of prominence over her brothers. The unfortunate results in many cases is that marriages can be little more than convenient arrangements for increasing the number of people in the extended family and may thus lack the rich mix of love, care and sharing the Bible envisages.

One of the more unfortunate demonstrations of this fact is the prevalence in both Zambia and Zimbabwe of what is called the dispossession of widows. In the event of a husband dying before his wife, relatives move in and strip the house of all assets, distributing them among themselves and leaving the widow and her children destitute. "There are many people who take the cattle or the money paid for the daughters of their deceased brothers, but do not provide the sons of their brothers with wives."[24] In an atmosphere like this, biblical teaching on subjects like marriage often falls on stone-deaf ears. One Christian with whom I discussed these issues said to me that one needs to live in exile, away from one's relatives and cultural milieu, in order to have any chance of being true to the teaching of the Bible in these matters. He at least recognized the challenge but indicated that attempts to be successful were doomed to fail!

Ukulilapo. Ukulilapo is a Bemba word derived from the word *ukulya* (to eat). It implies that in every situation it is my duty to exploit circumstances to my personal (and by extension my extended family's) advantage. The attitude may well have arisen at a time when eating was the preoccupation of most people, and feasting was desirable because it was so rare. However it came about, this attitude, and nepotism as an expression of it, makes public and social accountability very difficult indeed.

New orphanages are a case in point. Many of these institutions have sprung up in response to the great numbers of orphans from the scourge of the AIDS pandemic. The suffering of children attracts a lot of sympathy from donors all over the world. And yet it is common to see the children for whom such aid is sought and procured still languishing on scraps while the person running the orphanage grows wealthier, along with his or her relatives. Such abuse of public trust is understood not for what it really is—stealing—but as a duty. Dare I suggest that some of the resources of many local churches and denominations are misused in this way?

Life after death. God has put eternity in the heart of people, according to Ecclesiastes 3:11. Whatever else this verse means, it certainly suggests that it is part of the human condition not only to long for but to seek for life after life.

In Africa there are two clear lines of thought in considering what happens to a person after death. The first is the translation of the dead into the *living dead.* These are the spirits of the departed who are nevertheless very much alive and well, residing in the neighborhood either in a physical reality like a tree or simply as a disembodied spirit, and still part of the family. Care must be taken not to ignore or be negligent to them. Libations and foods must be left for them. In times of crises they can be consulted and appealed to for protection. Eventually they will pass on when their memory is completely erased from human consciousness after the demise of the last remaining relative who remembers them in physical form; from then on they become part of the corporate identity of the spirits of our fathers.

The second line of thought in dealing with the afterlife has to do with *inheritance*. After the death of a man or woman, the relatives gather to appoint the person who will inherit the deceased. It is important to establish that inheritance in this case has little to do with receiving bequests and everything to do with "becoming," in a mysterious way, the person who has died. Symbolically the family through the ceremony invites back the departed and renews contact with him or her.[25] At the appointed time a younger relative will be nominated. Sometimes the deceased might have nominated the person he desired. In matrilineal ethnic groups the line of inheritance goes through a man's sisters and their children, and his uterine nephews and nieces.[26] This is perhaps what makes the sisters of a man so special and important: they bear the boys who will take his name after his death.

The ritual is chaired by a leading member of the family, and all involved are asked to sit in the circle. The nominee is asked to sit in the middle of the circle and is given water to drink and token chattels from the wardrobe of the deceased. He or she may also be given some implements that defined the major activity of the deceased, for example, a gun if the deceased had been a hunter or a hoe for a farmer. Words are uttered, inviting back the deceased to take up residence in the body of the nominee. The nominee inherits a person, not wealth. As the ritual of inheritance unfolds, comments are invited from everyone who wishes to speak. The speakers address the nominee in words that make it clear that they are addressing the departed.

From that moment on the candidate in effect becomes the departed. This person will henceforth be the representative of the departed among the living. All who had relationships with the departed relate to the candidate in the same way. A man whose daughter has inherited his grandmother will always treat her with the same love and respect as he would his departed forebear. The children of the departed will regard the nominee in effect, and defer to him, as if he were their real father. Boys inherit their maternal uncles and girls their maternal aunts. The living dead are immanent and involved among their people in this way.

A friend once introduced me to his nine-year-old daughter with the words "This is my older sister." As long as the young woman is alive, and there are people who remember that she has taken the name of the departed, to all intents and purposes she is the reality of the afterlife of the person whose name she now bears. This is why it is so important to have children. A childless person is an oddity, and in the case of death peculiar rituals will be done to ensure that his spirit is not inherited. A childless marriage is no use to anyone, and the relatives will exert pressure to dissolve the marriage. All these expectations make for difficult teaching in areas of fidelity and faithfulness in marriage.

We can also speak of a third way of conceiving of the afterlife, which involves the naming of children. Names of the newborn are sometimes discerned through dreams and visions or divination. Such names will invariably belong to some ancestor whose spirit is seen to want to continue its existence in the material world through a newborn child.

These then are the three ways of conceiving of the afterlife, primarily in terms of the living dead or through inheritance but also by the giving of ancestral names to newborn children. Such an afterlife is bound firmly to this present earth, and existence in the afterlife is conceived of in terms of an earthly body. We might call this "existence by proxy." In more general terms we see the afterlife in a corporate disembodied spiritual existence as the living dead, a hope very different from the Christian hope.

The glory of the Christian message is seen not only in the resurrection of the new incorruptible body but in existence in the very presence of God eternally, without any fear of death (1 Cor 15:51-57). The preachers in the churches must take these values and look at them in the light of Scripture in order to be relevant to the African constituencies they serve. The repeating of evangelical platitudes originally conceived in other cultures will thus not serve the African church.

African concept of time. According to Mbiti, African time has two basic dimensions, the present and the past.[27] The future is important only in that it will become the present and later on the past. Time moves backward rather than forward. Time does not exist in a vacuum as something with independent value. Human beings create time to be used as it is needed. We are masters of time, not slaves to it (except in the limited sense of having to act quickly in the case of an emergency). African calendars, if they do exist, are phenomenological, filled with events and people, not a linear succession of measures of time leading to the future. It is the events and the people who define time.

The names of the months are instructive in this regard. In Bemba the names of the months correspond either to the dominant distinguishing human activity during that period or to the most prominent natural phenomenon during that lunar cycle. So November (*Mupundu milimo*) is not only the month when the mupundu fruit ripens but is also the busiest month in terms of preparing the fields for planting. June, one of the coldest months, is called *Cikungulu pepo* (the greater cold).

The Bible views time as something God created (Gen 1:3—2:2). It belongs to him, and through time he expresses his purposes and will. Time is not just the Greek idea *chronos* (a linear succession of events); it is also *kairos* (the appointed time), especially God's appointed time. God controls, interprets and terminates time.[28] The African view emphasizes our mastery and control of time, while Westerners view time as an independent commodity by which we are controlled. Both need to understand that without God our understanding of time lacks an important dimension. We are accountable to God in our use of time.

The good image syndrome. The seventh core value is *social definitions of truth*, what I call the *good image syndrome*.[29] Western philosophy since the Enlightenment generally conceptualizes truth in absolute terms but divorced from any metaphysical ideas or notions. This conception of truth has drawn a sharp distinction between facts and values. Facts are objectively true, while values are a matter for personal opinion. D. J. Bosch summarizes the debate in the following words:

Over against facts there are values, based not on knowledge but on opinion, on belief. Facts cannot be disputed; values on the other hand are a
matter of preference and choice. Religion was assigned to this realm of
values since it rested on subjective notions and could not be proved correct. It was relegated to the private world of opinion and divorced from
the public world of facts.[30]

Science assumes enormous prestige in this privileging of its form of
knowledge over biblical revelation. Scientific truth has its basis in observation, but observation has its limitations. A chicken observing the
farmer putting down food in its feeding trough assumes, on the basis of
observation, that the farmer puts down the food in order to feed it,
which is true but not the whole truth. The chicken has no way of knowing the financial and economic strategies behind the farmer's actions!
Nevertheless, in general it is observation that gives the Western concept
of truth the quality of timelessness or context autonomy. As a consequence, Western culture has basically rejected the metaphysical world as
true on account of such notions and concepts being unverifiable. Their
"truth" must be virtual rather than absolute. In line with this, a statement
is deemed to be true if there is a verifiable corresponding fact or reality
behind it. It is false if no such corresponding fact or reality exists. This
conceptualization of truth puts Western attitudes in sharp contrast to
those of other cultures like that of the Bemba.

For most, if not all, African cultures "criteria of truth and value are socially, not internally, generated and applied; responsibility is communal,
not conscientious, and public shame, not guilty self, is the penalty for
moral contravention."[31] When the need to tell the "truth" conflicts with
a greater value (e.g., the demand to protect one's "good image" or defend
a close relative), it is appropriate to tell lies. Although everyone acknowledges the lies as lies, the person who told them to protect his kin or his
"good image" will generally be upheld in the community as truthful.
This often brings much biblical teaching into conflict with culture.

I could add to this list still other significant core values: concepts of seniority and authority, guilt and shame, and so on. All these values are to be found in the spiritual core of one's life, the deep or foundational culture, and they form the integrating principle of life. They fundamentally affect how we view the world. They also affect how we perceive and practice Christianity for better or for worse.

Around such a core of values any culture builds its essential expressive or surface institutions, such as marriage and family, work, play, relationships, methods of healing, even the church; these human creations appear as the culture of any given people. The question is, how does the core affect the institutions any cultural group sets up?

Because the core of African values, which are spiritual in orientation, are in effect an integrating principle of life and because there is no secular-sacred divide in public and private conception of life, the core values affect every one of the essential cultural institutions. So, for instance, treatment of any illness is both a physical and a spiritual exercise. Unlike medical science, African systems of healing treat illnesses in a social context; the spiritual element plays an integral part. Similarly, priority of relatives encourages nepotism in public office and at the same time makes it difficult for marriages to attain the ideal spelled out in Genesis 2:24-25, where a man and woman must leave their respective parents physically, mentally, emotionally and spiritually in order to be united in an indissoluble union. The desire for children often means a person's worth is judged by his or her ability to bear children, so childless men and women are the object of great community derision. Childless couples come under intolerable pressure to break up.

What is the effect of these core values on the institutions of the church? Ideally, at conversion core values are "converted" and replaced by biblical values, derived from the Bible and enshrined in our hearts by the Holy Spirit. Because the core values are already both spiritual in orientation and an integrating principle in life, it is often stated that when an African gets converted, the core values are somehow transformed to reflect new allegiances and immediately, following established patterns, become the new integrating principle of life in its totality. The unavoidable inference is that the African church should therefore reflect biblical values through and through.

This is obviously too simplistic a formula. Processes of conversion are truly complex, and they occur for a variety of reasons quite apart from the straightforward desire to follow another religion. M. I. Aguilar says, "African processes of conversion are fluid, and they also include processes of reconversion to religious practices socially present in the eras preceding the world religions."[32] Fear, opportunities for commercial and political advancement, desire to create cohesion around a tribal identity and economic survival can play significant parts in the decision made especially by groups of people to convert from traditional beliefs to a world religion. Since core values change very slowly at the presuppositional philosophical level,[33] it takes a long time before "true" religion of the heart corresponds with what takes place at the expressive or surface level culture. In the intervening period we can expect to see a kind of localization of the new religion as expressive cultural forms superficially change to correspond to the newfound faith.

This is the case in much of Africa, where Christianity appears as a veneer thoroughly affected by the original African core values. "The Christian spiritual import, with its aim at bringing men to their ultimate goal in heaven may be a mere overcoat over traditional deep seated beliefs and customs leaving them undisturbed."[34] This I believe is the reason the church in Africa has so often been compared to a river two miles wide but a mere two inches deep! African Christianity has failed to root into the foundational or deep cultural level of the host cultures on the African continent. Instead it has adopted surface cultural changes, such as singing Christian hymns,[35] meeting on Sundays, reading the Bible, and adopting "Christian" names and forms of dressing, taking communion and undergoing baptism.

In this chapter I have attempted to show an African's perspectives on human nature. One thing that stands out strongly is the African sense of community. This value is close to biblical emphases, as seen in the use of collective metaphors to describe the people of God, such as the "body" of Christ. This obvious strength in the African experience also presents major challenges, for the church is often seen in competition with the family—and it is the church that loses out. I have explored the concept of deep and surface cultures by using a variety of metaphors taken from horticulture (the onion and its rings), architecture (the building with its foundation and superstructure), nature (the tree with its roots and branches) and geology (deep and surface cultures). In the next chapter I will make some general remarks about cultures and then look at how human beings can be reconciled with God, for without such reconciliation it is impossible to be the full human beings God intended us to be.

5

The Human Condition in the Light of the Gospel

HUMAN BEINGS ARE INCURABLY CULTURAL. Sometimes we pretend we are not bound by a specific culture or that we do not bear cultural identities. Many years ago in a remote part of Zambia I picked up a hitchhiker. He was conspicuous by the fact that he was white in a country where the majority are black, and by his fancy clothes. We struck up a conversation, and as we talked I suggested that his accent gave him away as a graduate of either Oxford or Cambridge in England, with certainly an upper-middle-class upbringing. He appeared to take offense at my suggestion, although he did not object to my associating him with Oxford or Cambridge; he told me in no uncertain terms that he spoke the Queen's English and therefore could not and did not have an accent!

The truth is, we all speak with an accent, whether we like it or not. That accent reflects the most prominent linguistic influences in our lives. I once heard John Stott tell the story of a Filipino boy who, having listened to him speaking, turned up his head and said to him, "You do talk funny!" Given that this encounter was in the Philippines, it was indeed John Stott who "talked funny." "Normal" people in the Philippines do not talk like that, even when they speak English! This may be referred to as "permanent mother tongue interference."

All human beings are incurably cultural or, as Turner puts it, "Cultures are inescapable and indispensable for human existence."[1] However, our cultures and the values they generate are bound in time and space. We are all culturally specific human beings. Globalization may create a global culture, but even that is nevertheless a highly specific culture.

> Culture is the self-expression of a group of people in time and space. It is an expression of life, a mode of becoming oneself, a way of relating to another and to nature. Culture thus embraces the wholeness of language, tradition, beliefs, institutions and customs that hold a community together. Culture is a complex reality that includes spiritual, material, intellectual and emotional features. The ethos, the self-identity of a people, is manifested through culture.[2]

Cultural values, and consequently cultural identities, are imbibed even as we were nursed as infants. Like a fish does not know it is wet, we are sometimes blind to the extent of our cultural specificity: "All human beings live within and by means of one or more cultures."[3] Sometimes when we leave our natural "habitats" and become exposed to other people's habitats we can begin to see just how different we are (the extent of our cultural specificity)—unless, of course, we belong to a missionary imperialistic culture (seemingly the case with my hitchhiker friend), in which case we see our mission in life as converting everyone to our way of doing things. This was precisely the way some early Jewish Christians viewed their mission in life. Thankfully, the apostolic council of Acts 15, having considered the matter carefully under the leadership of the Holy Spirit, decided against such a crusading spirit and "set the Gospel and the Gentile mission free from Jewish legalism."[4]

Eighteen hundred years later, however, the gospel and Christian mission would again be shackled, this time to the imperialist cultures of Western Europe at the high-water mark of colonialism. The mission of the colonizers was to Christianize and civilize. The Christian gospel became a tool in the hands of the colonizers and became trapped in the culture of Western imperialism. This was evidently the case with early Puritan missionaries to the Native Americans. They were given specific instructions to "make them English in their language, civilised in their habits, and Christian in their religion."[5]

On the other side of this same fallacy are young African Christians who say they recognize no culture on account of their newfound faith in Christ. What they really mean is that they reject the cultures into which they were born and brought up, presumably because they have bought into some negative imperialist propaganda that describes their cultures as primitive, demonic and therefore un-Christian (although it is true that some elements in every culture are demonic). Sometimes this attitude stems from a misunderstanding: since the gospel transcends culture, those who come under the influence of the gospel, it is thought, also personally transcend (live above) their cultures. In the place of their cultures they may adopt what they wrongly perceive to be "the Christian" culture—some mimicry of the Christian culture of a golden age such as the Puritan era. This was true of the Reformed wing of the Baptists in Zambia in the 1980s and 1990s. Pentecostal and charismatic counterparts in Zambia often preferred the more contemporary culture of Trinity Broadcasting Network (TBN), which is effectively the culture of certain parts of California.

Both approaches are philosophically and practically flawed. They reveal a basic ignorance about the nature and effect of culture upon a person, as well as a misapprehension of the fact that the gospel always seeks and needs to make a home in every culture. For example, although Jesus could have come into our world in an unrecognizable heavenly form, he chose a specific cultural form in time and space for his incarnation: he came as a Hebrew person. Jesus was not ashamed of his cultural orientation; he did not deny or seek to change it but encouraged his people to serve God in spirit and truth within that culture.

The enculturation principle is in reality the incarnation principle. The specificity of culture is not wrong in itself, although certain elements within any given culture may command what God has forbidden or forbid what God has commanded. Where these occur it is the duty of the believers to point them out and to show God's way. This may be costly, but it is part of the calling to faithfulness to Christ. It is the way we make sense of life and our self-understanding that is largely determined by our cultural lenses.

This is why it is important for Christians to be courageous enough to go with "Christ as he stands in the midst of Islam, of Hinduism, of the primal world-view, and watch with him, fearfully and wonderingly, as he becomes dare we say it?—Muslim, Hindu or Animist, as once he became Man, and a Jew."[6] J. V. Taylor did not mean to imply that Christ would change his historic Jewish nature to something else, or that historic Christian doctrines will be replaced by Muslim, Hindu or animist philosophies and practices. Rather, Christ needs to make sense to Muslims, Hindus and animists in the context of their cultures. Christianity among those who are culturally Muslim, Hindu or animist must express itself in cultural forms consistent with the host cultures. I take it for granted that the gospel will in time have its transformative influence on each host culture and thereby purge away those elements of that culture inconsistent with it. That is its prerogative.

INTEGRATING BIBLICAL TEACHING AND AFRICAN CULTURE

How then can we integrate biblical teaching and the various African cultures? It is important to be reminded that this is imperative, and the conditions are right for a fresh African theology to emerge out of the exercise of grappling with issues at the interface of Christianity and African cultures. Andrew Walls contends that "Christian history indicates that searching, fundamental scholarship arises naturally out of the exercise of Christian mission and especially its cross-cultural expression."[7]

Biblical teaching in Africa either is dressed in its original Hebrew or Greco-Roman culture, or has been transmitted to an African setting through another cultural medium, most likely Western (French, Portuguese or English). The process is not new. Already in the Old Testament we see a movement in which the Word of God works in and through a variety of cultures. The patriarchs lived within a basic nomadic culture. Jacob and his sons lived within a pastoral but settled culture in Canaan. Then for four centuries the Israelites were influenced by Egyptian culture. They maintained their identity and refused to be assimilated even when their children were threatened with death. In the eleventh century B.C. the nation moved from a tribal confederacy to a centralized political hegemony with the rise of the monarchy (a cultural adaptation based on a desire to be like the rest of the nations; see 1 Sam 8). Waves of colonial influence left their marks on the culture of the people of God. The professional group known as the Scribes and indeed the institution of the synagogue arose during the exile in Babylon and Persia. The entire New Testament was written by Hebrew people who used the lingua franca of the day, common Greek.

Quite apart from these macroshifts, there is evidence of foreign cultural ideas being introduced into the relationship between Israel and God. Three pertinent examples include the concepts of *covenant*, *kingship* (from the Old Testament) and *justification* (from Paul in the New Testament). All these ideas were culturally common before they were adopted and adapted to carry specific meaning relating to God's intervention in human history.

THREE BIBLICAL EXAMPLES: COVENANT, KINGSHIP AND JUSTIFICATION

The word *běrît*, translated "covenant," has very deep biblical roots. It is a fundamental element in biblical thought as well as in the national existence of Israel.[8] But before it became such a significant theological word, it was used commonly, not only in Israel but in the surrounding cultures in the ancient Near East, as a means of regulating relationships.

Covenants were common between conquerors and their vassals,

kings and other kings, kings and their subjects, friends, tribes and so on. Walter Eichrodt says that in time the covenant became "the concept in which Israelite thought gave definitive expression to the binding of the people of God and by means of which they established firmly from the start the particularity of their knowledge of him."[9] Eichrodt goes on to suggest that covenant is the lens through which to view the whole Old Testament, or the backbone around which to build an Old Testament theology. He may be overstating the case, but covenant did become a very significant means by which the Hebrews understood themselves in relation to their God. In fact, all God's relationships with his people have been regulated by one covenant or other.[10] But the word *covenant* and the concepts behind it were in common use already before these developments. As Louis Berkhof says, "Covenants among men had been made long before God established his with Noah and with Abraham, and this prepared men to understand the divine revelation, when it presented man's relation to God as a covenant relation."[11]

The covenant of grace. My first experience of the practice of covenant was something I observed among low-paid mine workers on the Copperbelt in Zambia in the early 1960s. Two men would covenant to give each other their pay in its entirety every other month. This enabled each of the men to have a relatively large amount of money in alternate months for the purpose of making significant purchases. The practice existed between people who regarded each other as equal partners; it depended on trust, and had considerable benefits for both parties. There was also risk and therefore sacrifice, but I do not recall ever hearing of a case in which the system was abused.

In Abraham's day, parties entering into a covenant would bring an animal, which they would proceed to kill and cut into two halves. The corresponding halves of the carcass would then be placed on the ground opposite each other, and the two parties would then walk between the pieces (see Gen 15:17). It is a matter of interest that Abraham was sent into a deep sleep while a substitute walked between the pieces, presumably because Abraham—not being an equal with God—could not enter into a covenant of equals with God. Later on God seems to remove all distance between them so that Abraham can even bargain with God on behalf of the residents of Sodom and Gomorrah (Gen 18:22-32).[12] The symbolism of cutting the carcass and walking between the pieces partly indicates what would happen to the party that defaulted on its commitments. The bond so established was in principle virtually unbreakable except by death. Certainly from God's point of view the covenant is eternal and can never be broken by him: the promises he makes contain the word *forever* (see Gen 17:19; Heb 13:20).

The Bible gives us examples of human covenantal faithfulness where no personal self-interest would be allowed to breach the commitment and faithfulness. Such faithfulness would continue even after death. A prime example is Jonathan's commitment to David, his friend (a covenant term). Saul (Jonathan's father) wanted to kill David in order to create a dynasty and secure Jonathan's future place as king of the nation (see 1 Sam 20:8-17, 30-31). But Jonathan protected his covenant friend from the plans of his father. For his part, when David became king he sought out Mephibosheth, the only surviving son of his friend Jonathan, and restored to him the lands of his grandfather Saul and his father, Jonathan. David also had servants work for Mephibosheth, who lived in David's palace and ate at his table in Jerusalem (see 2 Sam 9). There are some who think this was nothing more than cunning on David's part, so that he could preempt any likelihood of a rebellion, but it is more likely that this is the outworking of his covenant of love for his friend Jonathan.

In the biblical covenants God played a leading role in establishing the relationship. Because human beings could not stand on an equal footing with God, he took the initiative to enter into a covenant, and he set out the terms by which the human party would stand in relation to him. There is an obvious one-sidedness in this arrangement, but it could not be otherwise because the parties could not be equals. God's part in the covenant is not simply to show his benevolent character in a purely disinterested manner but especially to restore the image that sin has marred almost to oblivion. Ultimately it was the sacrificial death of the blood of Jesus that would make this blessing available for all people. In this God not only forgives sin by paying with the blood of his own Son but restores fellowship between himself and his creatures. The tragedy of Genesis 3 is reversed in the blood of Jesus Christ. Through Jesus Christ, God establishes a covenant with all those who come to trust him for salvation.

There are two basic elements to the covenant of grace. First, there are the *promises of God.* The basic promise, which encompasses all other promises, is God's pledge to be God to anyone with whom he enters into a covenant relationship. He said to Abraham in Genesis 17:7, "I will establish my covenant as an everlasting covenant between me and you and your descendants after you for the generations to come, *to be your God and the God of your descendants after you*" (my emphasis). In all the places where a covenant is either entered into or renewed (see Ex 19:6; 20:2; Josh 24:14-24; 2 Sam 7:8-16; Jer 31:33; 32:38; Ezek 34:24; 2 Cor 6:16; Rev 21:3) something like these words appears. This basic promise effectively puts at the disposal of covenant beneficiaries the resources of God and his name. Ultimately all the promises of lands, names, temporal blessings of a spiritual and material nature, forgiveness of sin, the indwelling of the Spirit, and a place with him in eternity are fulfilled and will be fulfilled, because he is their God.

Second, in relation to this divine initiative of love, there must be a *corresponding response* from the chosen people. This is what we see in the people's affirmation before Joshua in Joshua 24. They affirm that they will be God's people and will serve him faithfully and truthfully, and walk in his ways—the bridge between the fact of being chosen and the purpose of that election. God said that he had chosen Abraham in order that he might walk in God's ways, and then God would fulfill his promises to Abraham to be a bearer of blessings to all the families of the world (Gen 12:1-3; 18:19). Abraham's mission in the world—the purpose of his life, the reason he entered into a covenant with God—was to bring the blessings of God to the whole world, or rather to every person in the whole world.

It is easy to lose sight of this purpose. Many people take for granted the fact of being chosen, as if being a follower of Jesus is simply a badge of honor. It *is* an honor to be called a child of God, but there is much more to it than that. We are called to bear the good news of what God has done especially in and through Jesus Christ. Jesus made this clear in Mark 1:17, when he first called his disciples to "come, follow me, and I will make you fishers of men." Our response to God's call and the promises he makes involves bearing the blessings of his grace into the world.

In order to do this effectively it is important to learn what it is to walk in the way of the Lord. The way of the Lord describes God's characteristic behavior and our imitation of him.

> And now, O Israel, what does the LORD your God ask of you but to fear the LORD your God, to walk in all his ways, to love him, to serve the LORD your God with all your heart and with all your soul, and to observe the LORD's commands and decrees that I am giving you today for your own good? (Deut 10:12-13; see also Mic 6:8)

The chief characteristics of the ways of the Lord are summed up in the two words *righteousness* and *justice*. These are obviously big concepts, but they entail both personal integrity and social justice. But walking in the ways of the Lord for sinful people is not easy; in fact it is *impossible* (see Josh 24:19; Is 59:2; Rom 3:23; 6:23). Sin, which entered human experience through Adam and Eve, distorted and marred God's image in us but also made it impossible for us to walk in his ways. The promise of Jeremiah 31:31 hinted at a new work, in which God would write his law, as it were, on the hearts of human beings. This he has done in Jesus Christ, through which the image of God is being renewed in those who believe.

Jesus is the mediator of the covenant. There are at least two senses in which Jesus is rightly called the mediator of the covenant of grace. The

Greek word *mesitēs*, translated "mediator" and applied to Jesus and his work (see 1 Tim 2:5; Heb 8:6; 9:15; 12:24), speaks of two things.

First, it implies that on the one hand Jesus satisfies the just requirements of God in relation to sin, and on the other hand through his blood he is able to cleanse the guilt of human beings brought about by sin. Notice that this transaction, in which human beings are prime beneficiaries, is brought about by God's initiative and love. Just as was the case in the establishment of the covenant with Abraham, so also in Jesus it is God who takes the initiative: "For God so loved the world that he gave his one and only son, that whoever believes in him shall not perish but have eternal life" (Jn 3:16). Christ came with power to intervene, "to do all that is necessary to establish peace."[13] Jesus died on the cross so that the blood of the innocent Lamb of God would satisfy the justice of God, who punishes all sin. But at the same time, the blood of Jesus cleanses us from all sin (1 Jn 1:8-9).

Second, the word *mesitēs* is used in the more conventional way to imply one who mediates between two parties to remove a disagreement or to reach a common goal.[14] Jesus mediates between the one God and all human beings. The disagreement in this case lies in the fact that God is holy and all human beings are sinners. Holiness is to sin what fire is to stubble—the two cannot exist side by side. Holiness will always consume sin. God will destroy everything and everyone contaminated by sin (Rom 6:23; Eph 2:3). Yet a holy God and sinful human beings, in two seemingly irreconcilable positions, are brought together in Christ. In relation to human beings, Jesus reveals God and his requirements; he then persuades humans, by his life, teaching and example and the preaching of his apostles, to receive the truths he proclaims about God to enter into an everlasting relationship of peace with God (Eph 1:12-14; 2:14-18). This is what Paul means when he speaks about being "in Christ."

A new creation. In a number of passages in the New Testament Paul speaks about those who are in Christ as new creations. In 2 Corinthians 5:17 he says, "Therefore, if anyone is in Christ, he is a new creation; the old has gone, the new has come!" Perhaps the translation should drop the "he is" and simply read, "if anyone is in Christ, a new creation . . ." One implication of this statement is that when people enter into this relationship with God in Christ, God regards them as new and before too long people begin to change to become more like the image of Christ. The new creation is for real. The old creation—stained by sin that results in insensitivity to God, an inability to walk in his ways and inevitable judgment—is done away with, and a new creation filled with new possibilities becomes ours through the blood of Jesus Christ. The resulting state of being is described variously in the New Testament as "a birth . . . but also a new creation, resurrection, light out of darkness, and life from the dead. We were slaves, now we are sons. We were lost, now we have come home. We were condemned and under the wrath of God, now we have been justified and adopted into his family."[15] All this gives us not just a tremendous hope for the future but a whole new outlook on life.

The power of Christ begins to prepare us for eternity now. Paul says that we are to "put on the new self, created to be like God in true righteousness and holiness" (Eph 4:24). In conversion we have already received this new nature and put off the old one, but now our new nature begins to appear in this life. Our former selves—our fallen humanity, our sinful nature—is cast off, and our new nature begins to emerge; one day in glory it will appear perfectly.

Christian experience of salvation is based on two convictions. First, in the new birth we have received a new nature, a new creation. Second, we have received a new mind complete with new appetites in line with God's requirements. This new mind is constantly being renewed through the Word of God, the Holy Spirit and the experience of Christian fellowship. Our new nature is constantly renewed or made more in conformity to the image of God through the process of putting off old habits and ways of living, and putting on a new lifestyle based on the teaching of Christ.[16]

The Christian view of the human condition is distinctive in many ways, as described in earlier chapters. It takes into account the fact of God, whose holiness has been offended by human sin. The consequences of this offense of sin leads to death both in the physical and the spiritual realms. But the love of God has intervened through the death of Jesus Christ, who died to satisfy the righteous and just requirements of God's holiness and also to provide a way of dealing with human sin. Christ's blood gives us the opportunity to break free from sin and slavery to death. It gives us freedom to live life fully with the help of the Holy Spirit. This is not a temporal thing but lasts into eternity. God has made these provisions and calls all human beings to repent, accept Christ and embark on this new journey of life with him, a journey that will never end. Further, he calls his people to spread this good news and so fulfill the command of God to Abraham and of Jesus to his disciples: to be the bearers of God's blessings to the world.

Kingship. What happened with the concept of covenant also applied to kingship. The Jews knew and understood the concept of monarchy, although up until the time they asked Samuel for a king (1 Sam 8) they were ruled by Moses, then Joshua and finally the judges. Samuel was in effect the last judge as well the first prophet of his kind. But when the Jews adopted the concept of kingship (with God's seemingly reluctant permission), God spoke through Samuel to fill the concept with new meaning. Unlike kingship in the surrounding cultures, their king was to be appointed by God. He was to be chosen from among the Israelites; therefore he was one of the people, or more important, he was neither to entertain aspirations to divinity or priesthood nor to consider himself better than his subjects. The king, moreover, was to be accountable to God through reading and heeding the teaching of the Torah, God's Word. He was not to amass untold wealth nor have too many wives (Deut 17:14-20). It is of great significance that on this borrowed concept of leadership God finally built the promise of the Messiah King who was to take the throne of his father David and establish it forever. That, of course, is the Lord Jesus Christ (see 2 Sam 7:14; Is 9:6-7).

Justification. A third example comes from the New Testament, with Paul's use of the verb *dikaioō*, "to justify," from which we get the noun *justification.* Justification by faith alone is one of the rallying points of Reformed faith. This word and its cognates have a Greek background in both the organization of the *polis*, the city-state, and the law courts. It was the work of a judge to justify; that is, to acquit someone vindicated by evidence in a court of law. One who was not justified was condemned.[17] The New Testament, and especially Paul, borrow this word from Greek culture but fill it with peculiarly Old Testament background ideas. Paul uses it almost exclusively to describe God's work in judgment. He argues in Romans 3:20 and Galatians 2:16 that no person can be justified by keeping the law. Indeed in his view the very basis of sin is this ambition of human beings to fulfill the laws of righteousness in their own power. Only a person who has died to sin can keep the law. But this is an impossible situation. We cannot keep the law because we are sinners; we can keep the law only by dying, but by dying we are confirmed in our separation from God and are fit only for his judgment.

But God has devised a way for us to escape this difficulty; it lies in what Jesus said, and especially what he did on the cross of Calvary. Jesus died to sin that we might live to righteousness (2 Cor 5:21; see also 1 Pet 2:24; 1 Jn 3:4-5). God made the death of Jesus something that can be applied to us so that we become effectively as if we were the ones who had died on the cross outside Jerusalem. He died in our place and for our sake. If we accept this truth by faith and stake our claim in his death with all sincerity, then God in his mercy forgives our sin. He does not simply overlook it, as if it did not matter; he forgives it because Jesus died on our behalf. He satisfies the demands of justice through his mercy and his son's costly and sacrificial work on the cross. All who utterly trust Christ for their lives are then saved from the penalty of their sin and are made free and able to serve God—or rather, to discover the plans God has already established for them.

It is an incredible but true thought that God cares enough about you that when he made you he also set out a plan for your life that would suit you most. Sin has made most of us ignorant of what God wants us to do. In Christ we now have the possibility of not only wanting to know what God wants us to do but actually accomplishing it: to discover the plan for our lives and to fulfill it (Eph 2:8-10; Phil 2:13).

Have you discovered what God made you to fulfill? Paul and Jesus use the word *justification* to show that God's justice is not the contradiction it might appear to be (see Lk 18:14) but fulfills the concepts of justice (sin is paid for), mercy (God forgives all who accept the provisions for removal of sin) and sacrifice (the death of his Son, Jesus). All this is done in order that the sinner who trusts and exercises faith in Jesus may be justified. In fact Paul argues that before God no one can be justified, for *all* have sinned and fall short of the glory of God (Rom 3:23).

The wider implications of these examples are clear. We are to look to host cultures for the terms or keys that will unlock the meaning of God's Word for the people in those cultures. One of the most spectacular examples of this process in recent missionary history led to the publication of Don Richardson's book *Peace Child*. In the book Richardson describes the possibility of the gospel story arousing the wrong response. The Sawi people, who over the centuries had perfected the concept of murder, were not satisfied with the killing of another person but sought to do so with sophistication based on treachery. The Sawi people always seemed to be shedding the blood of others in feuds that never ended. To them the real hero in the gospel story was Judas, who had apparently ingratiated himself into the trust of Jesus only to turn against him in the end and have him killed. This betrayal was sweet to their ears.

One day Richardson witnessed the achievement of peace that involved the voluntary exchange of two living children, the "Peace Children." As long as these children remained alive there would be peace between the warring parties. This became Richardson's key for the proclamation of Jesus as the Peace Child. The key had always been there, and in due course it became evident.[18]

This story has at least two very important implications for mission work. First, each culture is a repository of the instruments of communication that will make sense to the people and will be in keeping with their cultural values. Second, it is imperative for missionaries to find out what God has put in the host cultures as the keys for the communication of his Word to the people in those cultures. This is the incarnation principle. Jesus said, "As the Father has sent me, I am sending you" (Jn 20:21). Indeed Jesus in his Great Commission commands his disciples to go into the world and make disciples of *all nations*. Disciple making must focus not just on individuals but especially on nations. The things that make a group a nation, such as language, dress, land, housing, distinctive shared commonalities and cultural institutions, must be the focus of our attention, for these must be brought under the lordship of Christ. Each nation will thus indeed bring to the body of Christ some of its treasures—to enrich believers from other nations but also to honor and glorify God.

One of the failures of the modern African church is the inability of its Western trained ministers to make significant inroads into their native cultures and to use them in ministry in a way that would be culturally relevant. Perhaps a sign of this failure is the often observed incidence of well-educated preachers and pastors using a foreign language, usually the language of instruction in their own training (such as English or French), when speaking formally to their own people. One of the ironies of the situation is that usually their interpreters don't possess formal (let alone theological) training! How can we expect there to be true communication under such circumstances?

Occasionally preachers find themselves in a situation that demands fresh thinking, which may lead to a defining moment for them and their hearers. I faced such a challenge sometime in 1999 at a Salvation Army retirement home in Ndola, Zambia. My assigned passage was the story of the prodigal son from Luke 15:11-32. I carefully worked at my exegesis and prepared what I considered to be a good sermon. This was not the first time I had preached on this particular passage, but the night before I was to preach, I felt uneasy. Somehow it did not seem right or appropriate to do a normal "good sermon" for this group. The members of this congregation were not about to start spending everything profligately—as a matter of fact, they had nothing. How could I use this passage to speak relevantly to them?

"Go back to the basics," said a voice inside my head. So I asked of the text, "What is the real issue at stake? What is the key that when properly grasped will unlock the way to a correct understanding of the parable in its original setting and then a realistic application within this given cultural context?" I pounced on the idea of inheritance. In those days, before a Jewish man died he would divide his wealth into equal portions— one for each of his sons plus one extra. The extra portion would be added to that of the eldest son, who in due time would inherit the family name and continue the family line on the family land. It was rare, though not entirely uncommon, that a man gave his bequests to his sons while he was still alive. In such cases the initiative would always lie with the father, not with his children.

In Jesus' parable, the younger son's errors caused great offense. He deserved the severest censure, not only from his father but also from the community. First he asked for his inheritance prematurely. Then he turned his wealth into liquid assets and squandered them through a reckless lifestyle in a far-off land, presumably among the Gentiles. He took value that belonged to the nation of Israel and squandered it thoughtlessly in a foreign land. Then, adding insult to injury, when he was utterly destitute, he dared to return to his father. As Jesus told the parable, it was clear to his hearers that the profligate son should have been driven out of the community for the shame he had brought upon the entire village. What he had done was too shocking even to contemplate!

But the father welcomed him and restored him to his former status as a son (and with celebrations!). By running through the village the father humiliated himself; to run he had to hoist his outer garments, thus exposing himself. He did so, presumably, not just to welcome his son but also to protect him from the jeering and vengeful crowd. The reconciliation and restoration was achieved by the love of the one person, the father, who had been most offended by the son's actions. Because of his love, he overlooked not just the material impoverishment brought about by the irresponsible and selfish actions of the son, but also the expected convention determining the way the son should be treated. Because he so loved his son he refused to rest on his dignity as defined by custom and convention. Hallelujah, what a father!

Zambians also have an institution of inheritance. For matrilineal groups like the Bemba, Kaonde, Lamba and Lunda, the inheritance goes not from father to son but from a man to his sister's son. What is inherited is not material wealth but the name of the deceased:

> When a man dies his name, kinship duties and his hereditary bow are passed on to his sister's son or to her grandson through a daughter. The heir actually becomes the dead man in a social sense: he adopts the kinship terms the latter used, calling, for instance, "maternal nephew" the person he would previously have called "brother."[19]

In this way, the "living dead" spirits of the ancestors continue to have a visible presence within the community. The inheritance is not a private family thing but involves the whole community. Until the 1950s it was common for an inheritor to be asked to take as his wife a surviving widow of the dead man. As Richards says, "In daily life a Bemba behaves with reticence and shyness before his mother's brother since he may one day inherit the latter's wife together with his name, his status and his bow."[20] What possible relevance can the biblical parable of the lost son have to this Zambian cultural situation two thousand years later?

At this point Western readers or others unfamiliar with African cultures must try hard to think themselves into a very different cultural frame of mind. Suspend your value judgments and try to accept the story as it stands in its own cultural setting. Imagine that a Zambian man is designated inheritor to his maternal uncle. The matter will only become relevant when the uncle dies. But in the meantime, the uncle marries again, his third wife. The woman is not only beautiful but is also about the same age as the nephew, the prospective heir. The nephew had fancied the woman himself before his uncle married her. But now that the chance to marry her seems to have gone, he comforts himself saying that it would be just a matter of time before the woman would be his wife anyway. He knows that when his uncle dies, as part of his inheritance he will inherit the woman. However, the nephew's desire for the woman becomes unbearable. One day he is so totally overcome by his craving that he persuades his uncle's wife to sleep with him.

As I told this imaginary story to my mostly octogenarian congregation, the electric atmosphere in the room was almost tangible. At the point when I stated that the nephew committed adultery with his uncle's wife, one old woman, who normally slept through the services and would never dream to contradict a preacher, actually interrupted me, calling me a liar. What I was suggesting happened in my imaginary story was unthinkable. Such a thing can never happen, she asserted. It is unheard of and would be a terrible shock to the community and a source of fearful curses upon the offender and his family. The horror felt by my Zambian congregation was similar to the sense of shock that Jesus' original hearers would have felt.

The occasion for me was a "eureka" moment in my attempts at being a communicator of biblical truth in the Zambian context. I had not only communicated biblical material, but the communication brought about a reaction similar to the reaction of the original hearers of Jesus. This surely is the challenge of any preaching, especially crosscultural preaching! That experience underlined for me the importance of understanding the Bible primarily through its own cultural eyes. By focusing on the issue of inheritance, I had got through to the old lady, communicating the true significance of the parable in another culture. Jesus' hearers would probably have reacted as she did, perhaps even calling Jesus "a liar."

I hope that after the old woman's initial shocked rejection of my imaginary story, she moved on to see that the father's forgiving love was even more remarkable, given the gravity of the son's offense. Understanding the cultural assumptions behind stories from the Bible can become the springboard and guide for translating or preaching the message into our own world.

The concept of inheritance as I have described it among the Bemba is capable of yielding other elements to help us better understand the teaching of the Bible. The apostle Peter tells us that God the Father of our Lord Jesus Christ, who is rich in mercy, "has given us new birth into . . . an inheritance that can never perish, spoil or fade—kept in heaven for you" (1 Pet 1:3-4). Peter is using a human institution as a bridge to greater understanding of what God has prepared for us in Christ. Just as birth into a human family enables a person to enter into an inheritance that has been prepared by the preceding generation, so birth into the spiritual family enables one to enter into an inheritance prepared by our Father God.

Inheritances, often of great value, offer hope of a better and more prosperous life, but such inheritances in the ups and downs of life on earth often spoil, fade, lose their value or become a snare for the benefactor. For example, many people who inherit homes from their forebears have to sell them in order to pay capital gains taxes. What was meant to please and benefit becomes a millstone. It is also common for relations among beneficiaries to deteriorate after the reading of a will. Similarly, the financial gains from a bequest can disappear owing to the vicissitudes of our financial markets or through plain robbery. Inheritances do not guarantee long life, let alone happiness or peace. In fact on some occasions inheritances may even trigger unhappiness, vulnerability to harm and other winds of ill will. By contrast, what God has prepared for us can never disappoint. It does not go sour on us, fade or spoil because it is kept in heaven for us. In order to enter into this inheritance that God has prepared, it is necessary to be born into his family.

The Zambian concept of inheritance is very different from Jewish and Western concepts. For us it is not the things we inherit that matter but the people; it is not the material gains but the relationships and especially the hope that such inheritance gives to the dying and the community they have left behind. So how can this be used as a bridge to teach about the hope of humanity? God created a perfect world, sin introduced rebellion leading to judgment, but in Christ God has prepared a way to heal the rift between us and him and thus has paved the way for a renewed or recreated humankind. How does the concept of inheritance help in understanding this fact?

One of the first things we must note is the fact of community. A child is born into a community, and that child gives the community and its individual members the hope of continuity into the future. I have already mentioned in an earlier chapter that a few years ago a friend introduced me to his preteenage daughter as his "older sister." He spoke about her in reverential tones and with words that indicated pride, joy and deference as only a Bemba man can give to his sisters, the bearers of his nephews. As long as this young woman was alive she would represent his deceased sister. Inheritance as a community act signifies hope not just for the deceased but also for the surviving community, which sees its hope in having children who will perpetuate the lives of the dead beyond burial.

The fear among Zambians that we might become disembodied spirits prematurely results in the imperative that all people and especially all marriages be procreative. This is the way in which we express our traditional hopes for eternity or, rather, a hope for perpetuity. But this hope seeks to do everything possible to prolong or perpetuate one's life and influence *here*. This is its major weakness; at some stage sooner or later this hope will surely disappoint. However much we dread the fact, owing to distance from the current generation and dimness of communal memory, spirits of the dead eventually will become disembodied. Disease can wipe out whole families and communities, thereby expediting a people's entry into oblivion. So long as the horizon of our hope is firmly fixed and determined by earthly factors, somewhere along the way that hope will disappoint. The apostle Peter in his first epistle offers us a better hope for our communities, one shielded from corruption. What is this hope and how does one enter into it?

Issues of eternity cannot be settled with solutions at the temporal level. This suggests that any purely human solution, whether African or Western, will be inadequate. Problems affecting eternity can be solved only by someone with an eternal mind and perspective. Peter points us to an inheritance prepared by God the Father, the Creator who inhabits eternity and thus has the ability and power to deal with the problems of his creation and to fulfill its longing for eternity. The inheritance he offers comes to us through a new birth. We all have human life and earthly inheritances through the procreative abilities and the desire for children of our biological parents, but the new birth Peter speaks of comes about when each person accepts by faith the work of Jesus Christ on the cross (see Jn 1:11-12; 2 Cor 5:17; Col 1:21-23). Just as when a benefactor dies, wills and inheritances become effective, so when Jesus died he opened the way for all, not just a few people selected by accident of birth, to enter into that inheritance prepared by God for those who have been born anew.

This makes a lot of sense and is especially significant for Africans, for we inherit Christ, a person. As Jesus himself said, "I will not leave you as orphans; I will come to you. Before long, the world will not see me any more, but you will see me. Because I live, you also will live. On that day you will realize that I am in my Father, and you are in me, and *I am in you*" (Jn 14:18-20, my emphasis). By putting on Christ we have the potential to become more and more like him. *Mpyana ngo: apyana na mabala* (the person who inherits, inherits even the characteristics of the

deceased). Non-African Christians might want to reflect on the significance of the following texts within such a cultural context: God "has
made us alive with Christ" (Eph 2:5); "Christ may dwell in your hearts"
(Eph 3:17) so that we may "grow into him who is the Head, that is,
Christ" (Eph 4:15). Or again, "Christ in you, the hope of glory" (Col
1:27), "your life is now hidden with Christ" (Col 3:3).

The transformation envisaged in the lives of believers is possible because in a sense we have become Christ, who is our inheritance. As a
result of our being in Christ, we now enjoy certain qualities of eternity
in Christ, such as forgiveness of sins, freedom from guilt and deliver-
ance from the power of sin and death and from the prospect of an eternity in hell. These qualities are real today, although they belong to
another dimension of existence that will be fully revealed only when
Christ returns. We experience them partially because we are in that in-
between state where the life to come mingles with the life we are going
to leave behind.

Paul gives us a glimpse of what it will be like when our bodies are
transformed to fit our new status. He shows us that one day what we
now enjoy by faith will become reality when our decaying bodies will become incorruptible, imperishable and immortal (1 Cor 15:35-54). Both
Paul and Peter show that this inheritance will not disappoint, because it
is designed by God and kept in heaven to be revealed in its fullness at a
future time determined by God. *Inheritance* then is a keyword for a
proper African understanding of what we are and have in God. We have
put on Christ and have an inheritance far beyond our wildest dreams.
Inheritance also helps us to appreciate who Jesus is and his role in God's
plans for the future of humankind: the one who died is the one whom
we have inherited.

This fact might have implications for evangelism and discipleship in
that it would be possible when people become Christians, especially
when this is done publicly, for communities of believers to initiate the
young believers into discipleship with a ritual not unlike an inheritance

ceremony. Significantly, and perhaps more controversially, anyone who has inherited Christ—in whom the Spirit of Christ lives—cannot inherit other spirits, whether these are spirits of one's forebears or any other spirits; Christ can have no competitors in his abode. This would spell, for African Christians at any rate, the end of inheriting forebears. But surely it is in this manner that our cultures will eventually be rid of elements that are in direct competition to the kind of allegiance our Lord expects of his disciples who deny themselves, take up their crosses and follow him (Mk 8:34).

In reconciling individuals to himself, Jesus also aims to draw together communities living in alienation and hostility to one another. In Ephesians 2:14-17 Paul says:

> For he himself is our peace, who has made the two one and has destroyed the barrier, the dividing wall of hostility, by abolishing in his flesh the law with its commandments and regulations. His purpose was to create in himself one new man out of the two, thus making peace, and in this one body to reconcile both of them to God through the cross, by which he put to death their hostility. He came and preached peace to you who were far off and to those who were near.

The barrier or the dividing wall of hostility Paul makes reference to is the division between Jews and Gentiles. The Jews on the one hand were God's chosen people; to them belonged the promises of God, couched in the Law. God had specially created the nation through a barren woman, Sarah, the wife of Abraham. This act of election or choice separated the Jewish nation from all the other nations of the world. But right from the start it was God's intention that the chosen people, the Jews, were to be a channel through which all the nations of the world would enter fully into the blessings of God (Gen 12:1-3).

God intended that there would be one humanity, one family of God's people, but the barrier had become fixed: the fact of election had become an end in itself instead of a means to an end. The Jews possessed the laws of God, from which the Gentiles were in practice excluded. The Gentiles were far off, not in terms of physical distance but in spiritual distance, from God. There were some individual exceptions who, through the process of proselytism, effectively became Jews, in every way taking on the "yoke of Moses," complete with circumcision. The law was a barrier in more ways, however: in reality it was impossible for *anyone* to meet its demands, and so it stood not just between Jews and Gentiles but also between all people and God.

In dying on the cross Jesus fulfilled the demands of the law, thus satisfying God's righteousness. But he thereby opened a way by which both Jews and Gentiles can enter into the blessings of God. Figuratively just as the Jews became one nation by passing from bondage in Egypt through the Red Sea, so also all who appropriate God's blessings through the death of Jesus Christ become one family. In the church we all have access to the Father through Christ and have become members of the household of God: we are brothers and sisters. In Christ all human barriers of hostility are done away with. We are to treat all people with the respect that befits bearers of God's image, and must treat all church members as brothers and sisters. The 1994 Rwanda genocide, in a country presumed to be one of the most Christian in Africa, is a denial not only of our basic humanity but especially of everything we are and have in Christ. In the church there ought to be evidence of a warm inclusive welcome for all. This is Paul's vision of the one new humanity based on Christ's work on the cross.

Other Bible writers, especially the prophet Isaiah and the apostle John, enhance our understanding of this view of a new humanity. In Isaiah 19:19-25 three groups of people are brought together: the Israelites, the Egyptians and the Assyrians. Traditionally the Egyptians and the Assyrians were sworn enemies of the Jews. But in this vision Egypt becomes "my people" and Assyria "my handiwork" along with Israel as "my inheritance." The racial, religious and national barriers are down between these traditional enemies, and all three groups relate to God in ex-

actly the same way. God has embraced Egypt and Assyria as intimately
as he has his own people, Israel. In fact Isaiah extends this vision to include not just the peoples of the world, represented by Egypt and Assyria, but also all of nature. Humanity will be reconciled with nature,
and animals will be reconciled to each other so that wolves will no
longer terrorize lambs, leopards will no longer eat goats, lions will no
longer feast on calves, and a little child will lead them all safely. All alienation will be a thing of the past in the whole of the created realm, as the
knowledge of the Lord will cover the earth "as the waters cover the sea"
(Is 11:6-9). John adds to this vision when he envisages a great multitude
of people that cannot be numbered gathered around the throne of God
"from every nation, tribe, people and language" (Rev 7:9). In the final vision John sees a tree in middle of heaven whose leaves are for the healing
of the nations, and God is present among his people (Rev 21:3; 22:2).

The human condition, as it affects each individual as well as whole
communities, in the visions of John and Isaiah will reach its state of perfection in unrestricted contact with a holy God. And there we will live
forever!

Notes

Preface

[1]The Bemba are a Zambian tribe that traditionally inhabits parts of the northeast between the Luapula and Luangwa rivers. The word also stands for the language of the Bemba, which without capitalization means "a lake."

Chapter One: Concepts of Humankind: Old and New

[1]From the story "Jacko's Millions," a documentary that ran on BBC 3, May 7, 2004.

[2]Ian Barbour, *Nature, Human Nature and God* (London: SPCK, 2002), p. 59.

[3]"First Cloned Embryo Yields Stem Cells," posted February 12, 2004, <http.//discovery channel.co.uk/>.

[4]Barbour, *Nature, Human Nature and God*, p. 64.

[5]Bwalya is a common Bemba name. Bemba names are not gender specific.

[6]Mt 16:26; see Peter Vardy, *Being Human* (London: Darton, Longman & Todd, 2003), p. 81.

[7]Vardy, *Being Human*, p. 89.

[8]Colin Brown, *Philosophy and the Christian Faith* (Downers Grove, Ill.: InterVarsity Press, 1969), p. 183.

[9]Ibid., p. 148.

[10]John Dewey, *The Influence of Darwin on Philosophy* (Bloomington: Indiana University Press, 1910).

[11]Chris Colby, "The Theory of Evolution," 1996, <www.talkorigins.org>.

[12]Barbour, *Nature, Human Nature and God*, p. 11.

[13]Richard Dawkins, *The Selfish Gene* (Oxford: Oxford University Press, 1977).

[14]Barbour, *Nature, Human Nature and God*, p. 42.

[15]David Smith, *Marx and Jesus in a Post-Communist World* (Leicester, U.K.: Inter-Varsity Press, 1992).

[16]Brown, *Philosophy and the Christian Faith*, p. 119.

[17]Leslie Forster Stevenson, *Seven Theories of Human Nature* (Oxford: Clarendon Press, 1974).

[18]Ibid., p. 52.

[19]*Bantu* is a general term used to speak of types of Africans who inhabit many parts of sub-Saharan Africa (the Bemba word *abantu* means "people").

[20]J. S. Mbiti, *African Religions and Philosophy* (London: Heinemann, 1969), p. 92.

[21]Ibid., pp. 97-98.

[22]Ibid., p. 99.

[23]Placide Tempels, *Bantu Philosophy* (Paris: Presence Africaine, 1969), p. 97.

[24]Richard J. Gehman, *Who Are the Living Dead?* (Nairobi, Kenya: Evangel, 1999), p. 68.

[25]Mbiti, *African Religions and Philosophy,* p. 18.

[26]M. Mnyandu, "Ubuntu as the Basis of Authentic Humanity: An African Perspective," *Journal of Constructive Theology* 3, no. 1 (1997): 79.

[27]A. I. Richards, *Chisungu* (London: Routledge, 1956), p. 29.

[28]Mnyandu, "Ubuntu as the Basis," pp. 80-81.

[29]Tempels, *Bantu Philosophy,* p. 108.

[30]Mnyandu, "Ubuntu as the Basis," p. 80.

[31]Tempels, *Bantu Philosophy,* p. 175.

[32]Mnyandu, "Ubuntu as the Basis," p. 81.

[33]There have been cases where a child's name is changed in early infancy; inordinate crying was seen to indicate that the ancestors had rejected the original, given name.

[34]Derek Kidner, *Genesis,* Tyndale Old Testament Commentary (Downers Grove, Ill.: InterVarsity Press, 1967), pp. 65-66.

[35]David Atkinson, *The Message of Genesis 1—11* (Downers Grove, Ill.: InterVarsity Press, 1990), p. 68.

[36]Richards, *Chisungu,* p. 125.

[37]Nelson Mandela, *The Long Walk to Freedom* (London: Abacus, 1994), p. 33.

Chapter Two: Biblical Perspectives on the Human Condition

[1]In chapter four I will attempt to apply this discussion to an African (Bemba) anthropology or view of human beings.

[2]Charles Sherlock, *The Doctrine of Humanity* (Downers Grove, Ill.: InterVarsity Press, 1996), p. 29.

[3]R. C. Van Leeuwen, "Form, Image," in *New International Dictionary of Old Testament Theology and Exegesis,* ed. W. A. VanGemeren (Carlisle, U.K.: Paternoster, 1996), p. 644.

[4]Louis Berkof, *Systematic Theology* (Edinburgh, U.K.: Banner of Truth, 1958), p. 206.

[5]C. S. Lewis, *The Four Loves* (London: Harcourt Brace Jovanovitch, 1960).

[6]Van Leeuwen, "Form, Image," p. 732.

[7]John Calvin, *Institutes of the Christian Religion,* trans. F. L. Battles, ed. J. T. McNeill (Philadelphia: Westminster Press, 1960), 1:188.

[8]David Atkinson, *The Message of Genesis 1—11* (Downers Grove, Ill.: InterVarsity Press, 1990), p. 36.

[9]D. J. A. Clines, "Images of God in Man," *Tyndale Bulletin* 19 (1968): 72.

[10]G. A. Jonsson, *The Image of God,* vol. 26, Coniectanea Biblica Old Testament Series (Uppsala: Almqvist & Wiksell, 1988), pp. 10-13.

[11]Van Leeuwen, "Form, Image," p. 644.

[12]D. J. Hall, *Imaging God* (Grand Rapids, Mich.: Eerdmans, 1986), p. 97.

[13]Ibid., p. 99.

[14]Calvin, *Institutes,* p. 186, quoted in ibid., p. 103.

[15]Gerhard Von Rad, *Old Testament Theology,* vol. 1 (London: SCM Press, 1975), p. 144.

[16]J. I. Packer, *Concise Theology* (Wheaton, Ill.: Tyndale House, 1993), p. 72.

[17]Karl Barth, *Church Dogmatics* III/1 (Edinburgh, U.K.: T & T Clark, 1958), p. 195.

[18]A. A. Hoekema, *Created in God's Image* (Carlisle, U.K.: Paternoster, 1986), pp. 70-71.

[19]J. I. Packer, *Knowing Man* (Westchester, Ill.: Cornerstone, 1978), p. 20.

[20]R. J. Foster, *Money, Sex and Power* (London: Hodder & Stoughton, 1985), p. 92.

[21]Francis Schaeffer, *Genesis in Space and Time* (Downers Grove, Ill.: InterVarsity Press, 1972), p. 22.

[22]Derek Kidner, *Genesis,* Tyndale Old Testament Commentary (Downers Grove, Ill.: InterVarsity Press, 1967), p. 50.

[23]C. F. Keil and Franz Delitzsch, *Commentary on the Old Testament: The Pentateuch* (Grand Rapids, Mich.: Eerdmans, 1976), p. 34.

[24]Clines, "Image of God in Man," p. 69.

[25]Harold Turner, *Frames of Mind* (Auckland, N.Z.: DeepSight Trust, 2001), p. 28.

[26]Ibid., p. 266.

[27]This is quite apart from the consequences of action taken when we are "out of our minds." Drug and alcohol abuse are commonplace and their effects at eroding the moral fiber of any society are clear for all to see.

[28]Richard J. Gehman, *Who Are the Living Dead?* (Nairobi, Kenya: Evangel, 1999), p. 158.

[29]J. S. Mbiti, *African Religions and Philosophy* (London: Heinemann, 1969), p. 176.

[30]Atkinson, *Message of Genesis 1—11,* p. 20.

[31]T. F. Torrance, *Christian Theology and Scientific Culture* (Belfast: Christian Journals, 1980), p. 107.

[32]Clines, "Image of God in Man," p. 101.

[33]Ibid., p. 96.

[34]Atkinson, *Message of Genesis 1—11,* p. 35.

[35]A. I. Richards, *Land, Labour and Diet in Northern Rhodesia* (Hamburg: International African Institute, 1995), p. 288.

[36]Ibid., p. 289.

[37]These comments by Richard Bauckham were made in a public lecture given at the Whitefield Institute in Oxford on May 20, 2002.

[38]C. S. Lewis, *Surprised by Joy* (London: Geoffrey Bles, 1955).

[39]P. A. Bennett, *A Missiological Analysis of Selected Bemba Proverbs on Marriage,* M.Theol. diss., University of South Africa, 1995, p. 72.

[40]Unity Dow and Puseletso Kidd, *Women, Marriage and Inheritance* (Gaborone, Botswana: WLSA, 1994), p. 103.

[41]Ibid., p. 14.

[42]John R. W. Stott, *Issues Facing Christians Today* (Basingstoke, U.K.: Marshall, Morgan & Scott, 1984), p. 234.

[43]Tertullian *On the Apparel of Women* 1.1.

[44]Clement and Jerome quoted in Elaine Storkey, *Men and Women Created or Constructed* (Carlisle, U.K.: Paternoster, 2000), p. 85.

[45]J. A. Clanton, *In Whose Image? God and Gender* (London: SCM Press, 1991), p. 22.

[46]A. I. Richards, *Chisungu* (London: Routledge, 1956), p. 50.

[47]Stott, *Issues Facing Christians Today,* p. 238.

[48]Richard Bauckham, *Gospel Women* (London: T & T Clark, 2002), p. 13.

[49]Ibid., p. 17.

[50]D. A. Carson, *Love in Hard Places* (Carlisle, U.K.: Paternoster, 2002), p. 13.

[51]Colin Brown, *New International Dictionary of New Testament Theology*, vol. 2 (Carlisle, U.K.: Paternoster, 1976), p. 539.

[52]C. E. B. Cranfield, *Romans*, International Critical Commentaries (Edinburgh, U.K.: T & T Clark, 1975), p. 131.

[53]J. P. Louw and E. A. Nida, *Greek-English Lexicon* (New York: UBS Publishers, 1988), p. 293.

[54]Derek Tidball, *The Reality Is Christ* (Tain: Christian Focus, 1999), p. 39.

[55]Ralph Martin, *Colossians* (Exeter, U.K.: Paternoster, 1972), p. 5.

[56]Ibid.

[57]D. J. Hall, *Imaging God* (Grand Rapids, Mich.: Eerdmans, 1986), p. 78.

[58]Barbour, *Nature, Human Nurture and God*, p. 79.

Chapter Three: The Descent of Man

[1]Meg Guillebaud, *Rwanda* (London: Monarch, 2002), p. 11.

[2]John R. W. Stott, *Christ the Controversialist* (London: Tyndale Press, 1970), p. 142.

[3]J. I. Packer, *Concise Theology* (Wheaton, Ill.: Tyndale House, 1993), p. 82.

[4]R. T. France, *The Gospel of Mark* (Grand Rapids, Mich.: Eerdmans, 2002), p. 292.

[5]Derek Kidner, *Genesis*, Tyndale Old Testament Commentary (Downers Grove, Ill.: InterVarsity Press, 1967), p. 67.

[6]Packer, *Concise Theology*, p. 83.

[7]Ibid., p. 84.

[8]R. L. Dabney, *Lectures in Systematic Theology* (Grand Rapids, Mich.: Zondervan, 1972), p. 307.

[9]A. A. Hoekema, *Created in God's Image* (Carlisle, U.K.: Paternoster, 1986), p. 143.

[10]George Carey, *I Believe in Man* (London: Hodder & Stoughton, 1977), p. 46.

[11]R. S. Anderson, *On Being Human* (Grand Rapids, Mich.: Eerdmans, 1982), p. 100.

[12]Geoffrey Fisher, *The Fulness of Christ*, quoted in John R. W. Stott, *Evangelical Truth* (Downers Grove, Ill.: InterVarsity Press, 2005), p. 72.

[13]Stott, *Evangelical Truth*, p. 74.

[14]Dabney, *Lectures in Systematic Theology*, p. 323.

[15]Leslie Stevenson, *Seven Theories of Human Nature* (Oxford: Oxford University Press, 1974), p. 41.

[16]Dabney, *Lectures in Systematic Theology*, p. 325.

[17]John R. W. Stott, *The Message of Ephesians* (Downers Grove, Ill.: InterVarsity Press, 1979), p. 73.

[18]E. R. Norman, *Christianity and the World Order* (Oxford: Oxford University Press, 1979), p. 63.

[19]K. B. Maxwell, *Myth and Ritual, Divinity and Authority in Bemba Tradition* (Ann Arbor, Mich.: University Microfilms International, 1983), p. 24.

[20]The designation "living dead" is debatable. Some scholars, like John Mbiti (*African Religions and Philosophy* [London: Heinemann, 1969], p. 83), accept the African understanding that these are truly the spirits of the recently departed relatives. Others, like Richard Gehman (*Who Are the Living Dead?* [Nairobi: Evangel, 1999], p. 177), contest this understanding, preferring instead to regard these spirits as another of Satan's deceitful schemes in which his minions masquerade as spirits of the ancestors. For the time being I will follow Mbiti in using the

terms as they are used and understood by the societies concerned, and make no attempt to evaluate the two viewpoints.

[21]Mbiti, *African Religions and Philosophy,* p. 83.

[22]The Lumpa Church was an indigenous church set up by Alice Mulenga Lenshina; see John Hudson, *A Time to Mourn* (Lusaka, Zambia: Bookworld, 1999), pp. 17-18.

[23]Clinton Arnold, *Ephesians: Power and Magic* (Cambridge: Cambridge University Press, 1989), pp. 52-56.

[24]Dabney, *Lectures in Systematic Theology,* p. 232.

[25]H. C. Hahn, "Anger," in *New International Dictionary of New Testament Theology,* ed. Colin Brown, vol. 1 (Carlisle, U.K.: Paternoster, 1976), p. 113.

[26]Norman, *Christianity and the World Order,* p. 76.

[27]Stevenson, *Seven Theories of Human Nature,* p. 42.

Chapter Four: A Traditional African Anthropology

[1]G. M. Setiloane's *The Image of God Among the Sotho-Tswana* (Rotterdam: Balkema, 1976) is an ethnological study of the Sotho/Tswana-speaking people of Botswana with a view toward encouraging the judicial acceptance of these cultures as fit vessels for the communication of the gospel.

[2]I will come back to the "facts" about Zambian men in relation to sexual matters when I deal with relationships in marriage.

[3]B. J. van der Walt, "Being Human: A Gift and a Duty," series of lectures delivered in Kinshasa, 1988, p. 30.

[4]Ibid., pp. 20-21.

[5]Harold Turner, *Frames of Mind* (Auckland, N.Z.: DeepSight Trust, 2001), pp. 74ff

[6]J. S. Mbiti, *African Religions and Philosophy* (London: Heinemann, 1969), p. 119.

[7]Turner, *Frames of Mind,* p. 75; see also van der Walt, "Being Human," p. 20.

[8]Mbiti, *African Religions and Philosophy,* p. 1.

[9]J. V. Taylor, *The Primal Vision: Christian Presence amid African Religion* (London: SCM Press, 1963), p. 26.

[10]Ibid., p. 22.

[11]Women and Law in Southern Africa Research Trust, *The Changing Family in Zambia* (Lusaka, Zambia: WLSA, 1997), p. 53.

[12]Van der Walt, "Being Human," p. 21.

[13]Taylor, *Primal Vision,* p. 72.

[14]Mbiti, *African Religions and Philosophy,* p. 16.

[15]Taylor, *Primal Vision,* pp. 103-5.

[16]Mbiti, *African Religions and Philosophy,* p. 166.

[17]It is widely believed that death, when it occurs, is always the result of the malicious use of magic or witchcraft; death is always both natural and unnatural; see ibid., p. 155.

[18]A. F. Walls, *The Missionary Movement in Christian History* (Edinburgh: T & T Clark, 1996), p. 21.

[19]Taylor, *Primal Vision,* p. 93.

[20]Ibid.

[21]Women and Law in Southern Africa Research Trust, *Changing Family in Zambia,* p. 9.

[22]Ibid., p. 30.

[23]Ibid., p. 190.

[24]J. A. Van Rooy, *The Traditional World View of Black People in Southern Africa* (Potchefstroom, South Africa: Potchefstroom University for Christian Higher Education/Institute for the Furthering of Calvinism, 1978), p. 19.

[25]Mbiti, *African Religions and Philosophy,* p. 152.

[26]A. I. Richards, "Some Types of Family Structure Amongst the Central Bantu," in *African Systems of Kinship and Marriage,* ed. A. R. Radcliffe-Brown and D. Forde (London: KPI/IAI, 1950), p. 222.

[27]Mbiti, *African Religions and Philosophy,* p. 17.

[28]Lenard Nyirongo, *The Gods of Africa or the God of the Bible?* (Potchefstroom, South Africa: Potchefstroom University for Christian Higher Education, 1997), p. 94.

[29]This material is based on a discussion in an M.A. dissertation I submitted to the University of London for a master's degree in social anthropology at the School of Oriental and African Studies in 1996. A fuller discussion exists there; here I summarize the essentials.

[30]D. J. Bosch, *Transforming Mission* (Maryknoll, N.Y.: Orbis, 1993), p. 266.

[31]K. B. Maxwell, *Myth and Ritual, Divinity and Authority in Bemba Tradition* (Ann Arbor, Mich.: University Microfilms International, 1983), p. 24.

[32]M. I. Aguilar, "Reconversion Among the Baroona," *Africa* 65, no. 4 (1995): 526.

[33]D. R. Jacobs, "Conversion and Culture: An Anthropological Perspective with Reference to East Africa," in *Gospel and Culture,* ed. J. R. W. Stott and R. T. Coote (Pasadena, Calif.: William Carey Library, 1979), p. 181.

[34]Louis Oger, *Where a Scattered Flock Gathered* (Ndola, Zambia: Mission Press, 1991), p. 231.

[35]For a long time, hymns could only be "Christian" if they were in the traditional Western linguistic forms and idiom.

Chapter Five: The Human Condition in the Light of the Gospel

[1]Harold Turner, *Frames of Mind* (Aukland, N.Z.: DeepSight Trust, 2001), p. 84.

[2]K. I. Aram, "The Incarnation of the Gospel in Cultures," in *New Directions in Mission and Evangelization,* ed. J. A. Scherer and S. B. Evans, vol. 3, *Faith and Culture* (New York: Orbis, 1999), p. 30.

[3]Turner, *Frames of Mind,* p. 23.

[4]J. A. Scherer, "Faith and Culture in Perspective," in *New Directions in Mission and Evangelization,* ed. J. A. Scherer and S. B. Evans, vol. 3, *Faith and Culture* (New York: Orbis, 1999), p. 3.

[5]Ibid.

[6]J. V. Taylor, *The Primal Vision: Christian Presence amid African Religion* (London: SCM Press, 1963), p. 113.

[7]Andrew Walls, "Christian Scholarship in Africa in the Twenty-First Century," unpublished paper, presented at a missions conference, May 2004.

[8]Joachim Guhrt, "Covenant," in *New International Dictionary of New Testament Theology,* ed. Colin Brown, vol. 1 (Carlisle, U.K.: Paternoster, 1976), p. 367.

[9]Walter Eichrodt, *Theology of the Old Testament,* trans. J. A. Baker (London: SCM Press, 1961), p. 36.

[10]See Gen 9:8-17 (God's covenant with Noah); Gen 15; 17 (God's covenant with Abraham); Ex 19—24 (God's covenant with Israel through Moses); Num 25:10-13 (God's covenant with Phinehas); 2 Sam 7:5-16 (God's covenant with David, through which we get the promise of the eternal Messiah); Jer 31:31-34 (God's new covenant with his people, widely believed to have been a promise of the coming work of Jesus and the Holy Spirit in a manner previously unknown).

[11]Louis Berkhof, *Systematic Theology* (Edinburgh, U.K.: Banner of Truth, 1958), p. 263.

[12]See Walter Brueggemann, *Theology of the Old Testament* (Minneapolis: Fortress, 1997), p. 571.

[13]Berkhof, *Systematic Theology,* p. 282.

[14]W. F. Arndt and F. W. Gingrich, *A Greek-English Lexicon of the New Testament and Other Early Christian Literature* (Chicago: University of Chicago Press, 1958), p. 506.

[15]John R. W. Stott, *Baptism and Fullness* (Downers Grove, Ill.: InterVarsity Press, 1975), p. 71.

[16]John R. W. Stott, *The Message of Ephesians* (Downers Grove, Ill.: InterVarsity Press, 1979), p. 181.

[17]Arndt and Gingrich, *Greek-English Lexicon,* p. 197.

[18]Don Richardson, *Peace Child* (Glendale, Calif.: G/L Regal, 1974), pp. 178-80, 192-206.

[19]A. I. Richards, *Chisungu* (London: Routledge, 1956), p. 39.

[20]Ibid., p. 155.

Scripture Index

John Stott Ministries

The vision of John Stott Ministries (JSM) is to see majority world churches served by conscientious pastors who sincerely believe, diligently study, relevantly apply and faithfully expound the Word of God.

For over thirty years JSM's Langham programs have helped burgeoning non-Western churches to balance *growth* with *depth*. Three key programs help majority world church leaders disciple their congregations toward greater spiritual maturity.

JSM-Langham Scholarships have enabled more than 120 majority world church leaders to study theology at the postgraduate level in the West. Upon completion of their degrees, these church leaders have returned home to train the next generation of pastors in their countries.

JSM-Langham Preaching Seminars gather pastors for instruction in biblical preaching and teaching. These seminars provide intensive training for pastors largely unschooled in Bible exposition, bringing greater skill and clarity to their preaching.

JSM-Langham Literature works with seminaries and Bible colleges in over seventy countries to give needed books to tens of thousands of pastors, many of whom before had nearly empty bookshelves.

You can participate in the global church. Find out more by visiting JSM at <www.johnstott.org> or contacting JSM at <info@johnstott.org>.